Coaching Softball Effectively

The American Coaching Effectiveness Program
Level 1 Softball Book

Steven D. Houseworth, PhD
American Coaching Effectiveness Program

Francine V. Rivkin, MS

Human Kinetics Publishers, Inc.
Champaign, Illinois

Library of Congress Cataloging in Publication Data

Houseworth, Steven D., 1955-
  Coaching softball effectively.

  Bibliography: p.
  1. Softball—Coaching. I. Rivkin, Francine V.,
1956-   II. Title.
GV881.4.C6H68 1985   796.357′8   85-7667
ISBN 0-87322-003-X (pbk.)

Production director: Sara Chilton
Copy editor: Olga Murphy
Typesetter: Sandra Meier
Text layout: Janet Davenport
Illustrator: Dick Flood
Cover design and layout: Jack W. Davis
Printed by: Thomson-Shore

ISBN 0-87322-003-X

Printed in the United States of America

10 9 8 7 6 5 4 3 2 1

Permission to reprint softball rules in Appendix A granted by the Amateur
Softball Association, 2801 N.E. 50th Street, Oklahoma City, Oklahoma,
and the Southern California Municipal Athletic Federation, Box 3605,
South El Monte, California.

If you have a good eye for detail you may have noticed something different
about the front cover. Examine the pitcher carefully. If you think she is
pitching with the wrong foot forward, guess again. She is actually in the
correct backswing position and ready to swing forward with the left foot.

Human Kinetics Publishers, Inc.
Box 5076, Champaign, IL 61820

Series Preface

Coaching Softball Effectively is part of the American Coaching Effectiveness Program (ACEP) Level 1 sport-specific series. The decision to produce this series evolved after the release of the ACEP Level 1 sport science course. In that course local youth sport administrators were encouraged to apply the information presented to the specific sports in their program. They were asked to identify the skills to be taught and the proper progression in teaching these skills. They were also asked to develop a seasonal plan and sample practice plans for their coaches.

The task seemed easy enough, but it was not. Considerable time is needed to carefully identify the skills to be taught and then to put them into a seasonal plan from which daily practice plans can be derived. As a result, the ACEP staff were encouraged to develop this information for various sports which we now have done.

The ACEP Level 1 sport-specific series is unique in several ways.

1. The emphasis is on *teaching* skills to athletes, not on how to learn the skills yourself, as in most other books.
2. The emphasis also is on teaching basic skills to beginning athletes. Often, they will be very young children, but not always. Therefore, the books in this series are developed for coaches who teach the basics to children from 6 to 15 years of age.
3. Careful consideration is given to the proper *progression* for teaching these skills. Information from the field of motor development is combined with the practical experience of veteran coaches to ensure that the progressions maximize learning and minimize the risk of injury.
4. *Seasonal* plans for the teaching of basic skills are presented along with *daily practice plans* for three age groups. Coaches will find these plans very helpful.
5. Drills or exercises appropriate for beginning athletes are also included.

Three other helpful features appear in each book in this series: A short history of the sport to help you appreciate the evolution of the game, a glossary of terms, and the rules of the sport are provided.

Practical, *basic*, and *accurate* were the guiding principles in preparing this series. The content had to be practical for beginning coaches and yet equally useful for more experienced coaches. Coaches did not need another treatise on the sport; many of those are already available.

Keeping this series basic was perhaps the most difficult task. Including more information about the skills to impress coaches with all the knowledge available was constantly tempting. However, we resisted because this is not what coaches of beginning athletes need.

Finally, accuracy was essential; thus, many expert coaches and sport scientists reviewed the content of the book to confirm its accuracy.

To achieve maximum benefit, the books in this series cannot be read in an evening and then be put aside. They must be used like a reference book, a dictionary, or a working manual. Read the book thoroughly; then refer to it often during the season.

This book and ACEP are dedicated to the purpose of improving the quality of youth sports. We hope you will find the books in the series useful to you in achieving that goal. Enjoy your coaching, and thanks for helping young people learn to play sports better.

Rainer Martens, PhD
ACEP Founder

Contents

List of Drills

# Preface

You may be an experienced or relatively inexperienced softball player; you may be a volunteer coach for a recreation league, a school softball coach, or a student learning how to coach. Whatever your background, you will find *Coaching Softball Effectively* to be especially helpful in coaching beginning players who are between the ages of 6 to 15 years.

Coaching Softball Effectively is a unique coaching book; its purpose is to explain in a practical and easy-to-use guide *how to teach* softball skills to beginning players. In the first section of the book, the Coaching Guide, softball skills are explained by progressing from the more fundamental features to the more advanced techniques. Included in these explanations are (a) *coaching points*, which indicate common errors and areas of emphasis, (b) *teaching progressions*, which indicate effective teaching strategies, and (c) suggested *practice drills*, which facilitate the learning and reinforcement of softball skills. The second section of the book, the Planning Guide, contains seasonal plans for teaching softball skills and practice plans for three age groups. The Planning Guide also contains information to help you prepare for games and evaluate what should be done for improvement.

Even the organization of this book reflects the emphasis on practicality and ease of use. For example, the numbering system for drills will help you locate specific drills easily and quickly. Drills are labeled according to the chapter and the sequence in which they are presented. You will find *Drill (5.3)* by turning to the Drills section in chapter 5 and locating the third drill listed. Each

drill is also listed by its name and number in the List of Drills at the front of this book. Use this list if you remember the name of a specific drill but cannot remember the number for that drill.

Additionally, several tools located in the appendices will help you understand and implement the material presented in this book. These tools are (a) sample outlines for developing your own instructional guides and daily practice plans, (b) softball rules as adopted by the Amateur Softball Association (ASA), and (c) a glossary of terms.

While writing this book, visions of my own youth sport experiences returned to me. My experiences in a variety of sports were probably typical of most young athletes. Some practices and games were fun; some were boring. Some of my coaches were very good at teaching me skills, and some were not. Reflecting back, the best coaches were not always highly skilled at that sport themselves. Instead, they were skilled communicators, impressing in my mind how to swing a bat level, how to keep the face of my racket perpendicular to the ground, and how to dribble a basketball by touch rather than by sight. These skills are remembered not because I have fond memories, or even a good memory, as my wife will attest, but because they are well learned and useful today when I play summer league softball, tennis on weekends, and basketball in my driveway. Our everyday experiences are constant reminders of the skills developed through youth sports.

This book was written to be as practical and useful as possible to help you be an effective communicator and to take the guesswork out of your coaching. Rather than your athletes *accidentally* learning softball skills, this book will help you make *certain* they learn softball skills. I hope you will study it carefully and apply the information you learn from it, for your players will learn the skills of softball more quickly and will enjoy practicing and playing softball more. As a result, you will enjoy coaching more, knowing you have done your best.

Steve Houseworth
Curriculum Development Director
Sport-Specific Program
American Coaching Effectiveness Program

The Softball
Coaching Guide

Welcome to Softball! You have joined the estimated 3 million other coaches who make youth sports possible in the United States. Whether you are a volunteer or a paid coach, you have the opportunity to make a tremendous contribution to the development of your young athletes. Furthermore, almost 5 million young people participate annually in youth softball, making it America's most popular youth sport.

People coach for many different reasons: Some coach because they love sports; some because they enjoy working with young people. Others coach because they have a son or daughter who will play on the team. These are all good reasons to coach youth softball. In fact, no matter why you choose to coach, taking the time to help young athletes learn softball is an important contribution to their development and, consequently, to your community.

So now you are facing the upcoming softball season. Have you coached softball before? Have you thought about what you plan to do? Have you ever worked with beginning players? Do you know how to teach specific softball skills? If the answer to any of these questions is no, then you will want to read this book carefully. If you are determined to help the beginning players on your team have a positive and successful softball experience, and if you take the time to study *Coaching Softball Effectively*, then you will be on your way to a successful season.

It is important for every coach to establish a coaching philosophy, for this philosophy will help you determine (a) your goals, or what you want to accomplish, and (b) how you will accomplish these goals. You may want to consider one of two major coaching philosophies: You might choose to emphasize winning as the most important objective, or you might stress participation, fun, and skill development as the most important objective.

The philosophy we advocate through the American Coaching Effectiveness Program is *Athletes First—Winning Second*. By this statement we mean that every decision you make as a coach should first be in the best interest of your athletes, and second in the desire to win. We hope that helping young people to develop physically, psychologically, and socially will always be more important to you as you coach than beating the other team.

Athletes First—Winning Second does not mean winning is unimportant, or said more accurately, that striving to win is unimportant. You should instill in your players a desire to win, to strive to do their best, to pursue excellence. However, the outcome of the game—the winning or losing—is not the most important objective. The most important objective is that your players try to win, that they try their best. If they do their best, they will have been successful—regardless of the outcome of the contest.

This philosophy also will be reflected in how you present yourself to the players on your team. As a coach, you are in an influential position. Thus, *how* you teach will be as important as *what* you teach. To implement the ACEP philosophy, consider the following points:

Be a good role model. Present a model for behavior you want your athletes to emulate. Set positive examples at practices and games.

Everyone is important. Treat each player as an important human being. Each player will have a different personality and different needs. Be sensitive to these differences and show interest and concern for each team member.

Consider the age and skill levels of your players. Your athletes will be full of energy and eager to try many skills. However, they are also young and not yet capable of performing as adults. This means you must approach your athletes at *their* level. Do not expect them to come up to your level.

Consider individual differences. Teach beginning softball skills according to the ability of each player. Some players will be fast learners with whom you can progress rapidly. Other players will not learn as quickly, so you will need to proceed more slowly with them.

Keep everyone active. Organize your practices and games so that each player is able to participate as much as possible. Young players want to play softball for many reasons, one of the most important being to have fun participating. If they are not kept active in practices or allowed to play in games, they will quickly lose interest.

Include athletes in the decision-making process. Young athletes should have input as to what skills they practice and as to how they practice them. Ask your players what they need to work on, how they want to be grouped for practice, and what positions they would like to play. Naturally, young athletes should not control the entire practice, but do consider their interests and ideas when designing practices and playing games.

Be patient. You will need to have patience with beginning players who are learning softball. Softball skills require timing, coordination, and glove control that can only be developed through repeated practice. Encourage your players to develop their skills, and positively reinforce players for their effort and skill development. When young players learn new skills, both you and your players should be proud.

Part I: Offensive Play

Your players will enjoy hitting balls, running the bases, and scoring runs. It is a deeply satisfying feeling to hit a solid line drive to centerfield and to reach base safely. But your players must also be prepared to experience striking out, hitting into a double play, and being thrown out while attempting to stretch a single into a double. Being put out will not be much fun, but it is part of the game. You will need to help beginning players understand that reaching a base safely does not happen every time they bat. Helping your players develop realistic goals about their offensive achievements is as important as teaching them basic offensive skills.

This part presents the offensive skills of hitting and baserunning and explains how to teach these skills to your softball players more effectively. By following the techniques, teaching strategies, and drills listed in this section, you will help your players increase the fun of hitting, running, and scoring; you will also help them from becoming too discouraged when they are put out.

Chapter 1: Batting

Introduction: Hitting the Ball

Hitting a softball is a difficult skill for adults and even more so for children. Young people must develop the hand-eye coordination and the visual judgment skills necessary to hit a pitched softball. Hitting can be highly enjoyable when this skill is well developed, but can be frustrating when it is not. To help you teach these hitting skills properly, the following topics are explained in this chapter:

- The bat
- The grip
- The stance
- The swing
- Conditioning exercises for batting
- Bunting
- Batting drills

Several drills which will help your players practice effective batting mechanics are the Swinging in Front of a Mirror Drill (1.1), the Wiffle or Sock Ball on a String Drill (1.2), the Hitting off a Tee Drill (1.3), the Swinging a Bat Drill (1.4), and the Hitting Easy Pitches Drill (1.5).

The Bat

Present the bat to your players and explain that it is divided into three parts: the *knob*, the *handle*, and the *barrel* as illustrated in Figure 1-1.

Tell your athletes that bats usually have a number printed on the end of the knob which indicates the length (in inches) of the bat. For wooden bats, this number is also a good indica-

Fig. 1-1

KNOB   HANDLE   BARREL

tion of the bat's weight. For example, if a wooden bat has the number 28 stamped on the end of the knob, this means the bat is 28 in. long and will probably be close to 28 oz in weight. Metal bats will have the length stamped on the end of the knob or on the barrel of the bat. However, the length of a metal bat does not always indicate its weight. Be sure you instruct your players to look for the printed weight and length when selecting metal bats.

Bat Safety

Bats, of course, must be safe. Amateur Softball Association Rules state the bat should be all-wood or all-metal. Wooden bats should be hardened and finished, not rough. Metal bats must be one piece or have a plug in the barrel end. If a bat does not have a plug in the end, it is dangerous and should not be used, not even in practices. The knob on a metal bat should be a continuation of the handle. Some older metal bats have a rubber knob plugged into the handle; this type of bat is illegal, unsafe, and should *never* be used. The distinctions between legal and illegal metal bats are shown in Figure 1-2.

Selecting the Proper Bat

Help your players select bats that are the proper length and weight for their body size and

Fig. 1-2

LEGAL BAT

ONE PIECE CONSTRUCTION   END PLUG

ILLEGAL BAT

PLUG HANDLE   NO END PLUG

strength (see Figure 1-3). The most important selection criterion is that the bat feels comfortable and is easy to swing. Tell your players the length and weight of a bat will affect their swing: A heavy bat may cause a slow, jerky swing; a bat which is too light may cause an early swing.

The Grip

After helping your players select the bat, demonstrate how to use it properly. First, teach your players how to grip the bat. Show them to grip the bat as if they were shaking hands with it: Right-handed hitters place the left hand against the knob, with the right hand on top of the left hand; left-handed hitters place the right hand against the knob, with the left hand on top of the right hand. The bat should fit in the hands comfortably but firmly, with the fingers spread slightly apart and the thumbs at the top of each hand as shown in Figure 1-4.

Fig. 1-3

Fig. 1-4

LEFT-HANDED BATTER

RIGHT-HANDED BATTER

Choking Up on the Bat

Batters may gain more control by *choking up* on the bat, which means moving the batter's grip up on the handle, or toward the barrel end. Choking up will help those players who lack sufficient strength to swing the bat quickly and accurately. It is doubtful that the bats provided to you will be the ideal size and weight for all of your players, so many of them will need to choke up. Players can choke up slightly or quite a bit, as shown in Figure 1-5. Teach each player how to choke up and let each one find the grip which works best.

Fig.   1-5

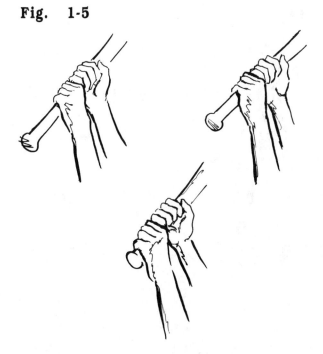

Coaching Points for the Grip

1. Shake hands with the bat.
2. Grip the bat with both hands close together.
3. Grip the bat firmly, yet keep it flexible.
4. Adjust the grip by choking up on the bat handle.

The Stance

The *stance*, or the position the batter takes when in the batter's box, is the next step in teaching good hitting skills. This is the foundation of hitting and must be mastered in order to hit well. The stance has many components and should be taught simply, especially to beginning players who are just learning the game. The simpler and clearer the explanation, the easier it will be to master the stance.

Selecting a Batting Stance

The *open*, *closed*, and *square* stances are the three general batting stances used in softball (see Figure 1-6). In an *open* stance, the batter stands with the front foot toward the outside of the batter's box. This stance can help batters in three ways. First, because the front foot is positioned toward the outside of the batter's box, the open stance helps batters who tend to step toward the inside of the batter's box by forcing the front foot to step more toward the pitcher than home plate. Second, the open stance helps batters contact the ball earlier, or sooner, than other stances. This means the open stance is useful when batting against fast pitchers, or when the batter has a relatively late (slow) swing. Third, this stance helps batters hit the ball along the baseline from the side which they bat (e.g., right-handed batters hit along the third baseline; left-handed batters hit along the first baseline).

The *closed* stance positions the front foot toward the inside of the batter's box and is used for the opposite reasons the open stance is used. First, the closed stance will help correct batters who tend to step toward the outside of the batter's box. Second, this stance helps batters who swing too early (fast) or who face a relatively slow pitcher. Third, the closed stance will help batters "pull" the ball or hit toward the opposite field from which they bat (e.g., a right-handed batter pulls toward right field; a left-handed batter pulls toward left field).

The most desirable batting stance is the *square* stance. In this stance, the feet are aligned and the toes point squarely toward home plate, and the batter steps directly toward the pitcher rather than toward the outside or inside of the batter's box. This stance is useful for players who have a well-timed batting swing and who want

Fig.   1-6

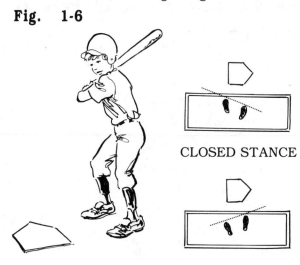

CLOSED STANCE

SQUARE STANCE   OPEN STANCE

to hit the ball toward the middle part of the field (between the shortstop's and the second baseman's positions).

Most beginning players wil not use the same stance each time, so you will need to watch your players closely and alter ineffective stances. Also some players may naturally use an open or closed stance, so let your players try batting in the stance which is most natural to them. If they have difficulty hitting from their natural stance, you can then help them adjust the stance until they are able to hit well. When you alter a player's stance, do not use an exaggerated open or closed position. This would be uncomfortable and probably cause more problems than it solves. Instead, alter the batting position bit by bit until your player can bat effectively.

The Shoulders and Arms

The position of the shoulders and arms will naturally follow the position of the feet. For example, an open stance will cause the shoulders to be open, and a closed stance will cause the shoulders to be closed as illustrated in Figure 1-7.

Regardless of the stance used, the arms need to be held comfortably back, about shoulder height, and slightly away from the shoulders. From this position it is difficult to rest the bat on the back shoulder, which is a bad habit and should be discouraged.

The Head and Eyes

Unless your players are lucky, they will not hit what they cannot see. It will help for you to

Fig.   1-7

Fig.   1-8

demonstrate how to watch the ball throughout the swing (see Figure 1-8). Jerking the head as the batter starts the swing is a frequent cause of batters not following the ball as it approaches the plate.

Position in the Batter's Box

Whatever stance your batters choose, have them stand back in the box so their front foot is even with the back corner of home plate, and they can touch the far front corner with the bat (see Figure 1-9). Standing back in the batter's box increases

Fig.   1-9

the chance of hitting the ball because the batter has a little more time to react to the pitch. Of course, this position should be adjusted as your players acquire a "feel" for batting, according to the speed of each pitcher, and to where the batter wants to hit the ball.

Coaching Points for the Stance

1. Stand about hip-width apart and square to the plate.
2. Stand away from the plate so that the bat touches the far corner.
3. Stand back in the batter's box, with the front foot even with the back corner of home plate.
4. Hold the shoulders square and the arms comfortably back.
5. Watch the ball.

The Swing

Now you are ready to explain the three phases of the batting swing: the *stride*, the *arm rotation*, and the *follow-through*. To hit a ball with a slender bat, these movements must be precisely timed and coordinated. Also, because the swing is a difficult skill to teach, be patient with your players and practice the drills suggested in this chapter, including the Batting/Fielding Drill

(1.6) which is helpful for practicing the batting swing in game situations.

Stride

Beginning softball players often think the most important part of batting is swinging the bat with their arms. However, because the stride moves the body into a swinging position, it is equally as important as the swing.

During the stride, the front foot steps toward the pitcher, and the body weight shifts forward, providing the batter power to hit the ball. This stride does not need to be long. A stride of 6 to 12 in., as shown in Figure 1-10, is all your batters need in order to hit the ball with power. Be sure to emphasize that the stride is a smooth and deliberate step, not a fast or jerky one.

The Arm Motion

When the front foot is planted, the stride ends and the forward arm swing begins: The arms should swing the bat smooth and level as the hips and chest turn toward the pitcher (see Figure 1-11).

When demonstrating the arm swing, show how to extend the arms (straighten the elbows), for some players may tend to keep their elbows bent. Explain that if the elbows are bent, the bat will probably not reach across the plate to hit the ball and that it will be difficult to swing the bat level or with power.

Fig.   1-10

STRIDE 6 TO 12 INCHES

Fig. 1-11

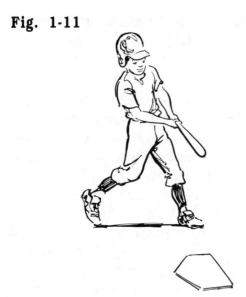

The Wrist Action

Wrist action is an important part of the batting swing, although because it is a natural part of the swing, it should be presented and practiced slowly. For proper wrist action, the wrists should rotate or "break" in the middle of the swing, as shown in Figure 1-12. Demonstrate how this breaking of the wrists occurs as the bat contacts the ball. Practicing the Wrist Roller Drill (1.7) located at the end of this chapter will help batters learn to rotate their wrists and develop good arm swing.

Contacting the Ball

The arm motion does not end with the bat hitting the ball; your players should try to hit *through* the ball. Hitting through the ball means

Fig. 1-12

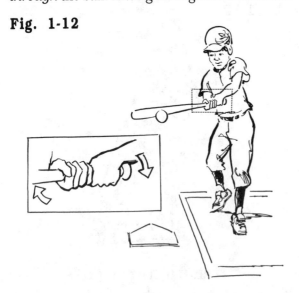

trying to slice the ball in half so that the bat will be on the other side of the ball.

The Follow-Through

The follow-through is the final part of the swing and is the result of a good stride and proper arm action. During this phase, the wrists continue to rotate, the arms swing across the body, and the hips twist fully around (see Figure 1-13). Sometimes players are afraid to swing hard, or hit through the ball because they do not know how to follow through properly, and the bat hurts the arm or shoulder when it comes around. By developing a proper follow-through, batters can hit through the ball powerfully without hurting the arms.

Coaching Points for the Swing

1. Stride with the front foot 6 to 12 in. toward the pitcher.
2. Focus the eyes on the ball.
3. Swing the arms level.
4. Swing through the ball.
5. Follow-through.

Teaching Progression for the Swing

1. Teach the stride.
2. Combine the stride with the arm swing.
3. Combine the stride, arm swing, and follow-through.

Fig. 1-13

Conditioning Exercises for Batting

Having the strength to swing bats and hit softballs effectively is important for several reasons: Insufficient strength to grip the bat firmly and swing the bat correctly will impair a player's ability to learn batting skills effectively and, thus, increase the chance for injury. To bat effectively, batters need a combination of leg, trunk, and arm strength. Study and use the following conditioning exercises we have selected to help your beginning softball players develop the strength needed to bat well.

Bat Lifts

Have your players grip a bat with the hand right above the knob and hold it out in front of the body. Then move the bat up and down with the wrists only, as shown in Figure 1-14. This is also a good exercise to demonstrate choking up, because if a bat is too heavy, the player can choke up, making it easier to lift.

Squeezing Tennis Balls

Players can develop grip strength by squeezing tennis balls, racquet balls, or any other soft, rubber balls. Because both hands are used in batting, be sure to exercise both hands.

Fig. 1-14

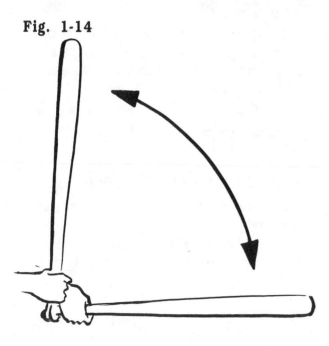

Resistance Arm Swings

Have players work in pairs, as shown in Figure 1-15. One player swings a bat against the resistance of a partner who holds the bat. The player swinging the bat should start in the ready position and swing the bat while the other player applies resistance. The amount of resistance depends upon the strength of the batter. Apply just enough resistance to make the batter work without disrupting his or her form.

Bat Weights

Another method of improving batting strength is to use a bat weight. Bat weights can be slipped over a bat to increase resistance during the swing and to develop strength. Because a weighted bat may alter a batter's swing, emphasize using proper hitting technique when swinging a weighted bat; also, make sure the bat weights will not fly off.

Hip Twists

This exercise will be fun and beneficial to your players. They should stand with their legs about hip-width apart, hands interlocked behind the head, and twist their body from side to side, as shown in Figure 1-16.

General Exercises

In addition to the exercises listed above, general conditioning exercises such as push-ups and sit-ups will help your players develop strength in the shoulders and stomach. These general conditioning exercises are useful because the muscles of

Fig. 1-15

Fig. 1-16

Fig. 1-17   Fig. 1-18   Fig. 1-19

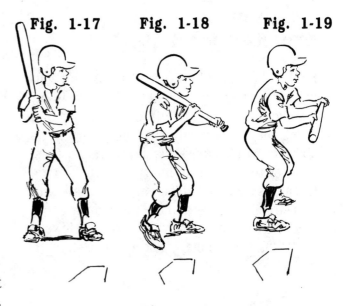

the shoulders and stomach are used to support and to stabilize the arms and body when batting.

Fig. 1-20

Bunting

Explain to your players that bunting is a way to hit the ball very softly. Bunting is not an easy skill for beginning players, but it is effective because the ball is hit slowly, causing fielders to run in to field the ball rather than waiting for the ball to come to them. To help your players learn this difficult but effective skill, follow the coaching points and teaching progressions presented below and practice by using a drill such as the Bunt Drill (1.8). Remember, bunting is allowed only in *fast-pitch* softball.

How to Bunt

You can demonstrate and teach the bunt, as shown in Figures 1-17 to 1-20 by (a) turning from the batting stance to face the pitcher squarely (be sure both feet remain inside the batter's box), (b) sliding the top hand up to the barrel of the bat, (c) holding the bat with the top hand between the thumb and the index finger (with all other fingers bent behind the bat), and (d) placing the bat in a level position in front of the pitch. Tell your players to bunt softly, as if trying to catch the ball with the bat.

Placing the Bunt

As your players become more proficient at bunting, encourage them to "place" bunts by learning to direct the ball to a specific area. For example, to bunt toward third base, the bat should be turned toward third base; to bunt toward first base, the bat should be turned toward first base (see Figure 1-21).

Coaching Points for the Bunt

1. Be sure the batter is in a square stance facing the pitcher.
2. Check the grip. The lower hand should grip the handle; the upper hand should grip the

Fig. 1-21

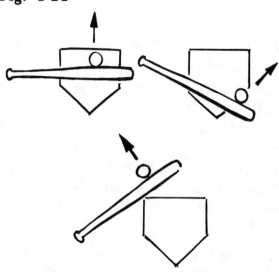

barrel of the bat between the thumb and the forefinger.

3. Be sure the bunter holds the bat level with the ground.
4. Raise and lower the bat by moving up and down with the legs.
5. Emphasize trying to catch the ball with the bat.

Teaching Progression for the Bunt

1. Demonstrate and practice how to hold the bat in a bunt position.
2. Teach your players how to square up to the pitcher from the batting position and assume the bunt position.
3. Practice bunting easy pitches from a moderate distance.
4. Gradually progress to bunting balls thrown at regular pitching speed from the regulation pitching distance.
5. Practice placing bunts.
6. Practice bunting under game conditions.

Batting Drills

(1.1) Swinging in Front of a Mirror Drill

Age: 9 years and up

Purpose: To allow players to observe their batting mechanics

Equipment: Mirror, bats (optional—can be performed at home without bats)

Procedure: Players stand in front of a mirror and swing as if hitting a ball. Instruct them to concentrate on the position of their arms, legs, head, and shoulders.

(1.2) Whiffle or Sock Ball on a String Drill

Age: 9 years and up

Purpose: To help your players learn to keep their heads still and their eyes on the ball when swinging

Equipment: Bat, whiffle ball, or sock ball (old socks tied into knots the size of a ball), a softball tied to a rope

Procedure: Suspend the sock ball or ball on a rope from a garage ceiling, backstop overhang, or any other apparatus which will allow your players to swing at the ball without interference. Players get into the ready position and practice hitting the ball correctly.

(1.3) Hitting off a Tee Drill

Age: All

Purpose: To develop the mechanics of players' swings using a stationary ball

Equipment: Batting tee, bats, softballs, home plates

Procedure: Your players can construct a "hitting laboratory" in a garage or on the field. Balls can be hit into a net, tarp, sheet, backstop, or blanket draped from the ceiling. Place the balls on the hitting tee and practice the batting swing.

(1.4) Swinging a Bat Drill

Age: All

Purpose: To develop and to refine a player's batting swing

Equipment: A bat (optional)

Procedure: Demonstrate how to (a) stride, (b) swing, and (c) follow through without the bat.

Have your players practice these three phases and give them correct, precise feedback to correct errors.

(1.5) Hitting Easy Pitches Drill

Age: All

Purpose: To practice hitting a pitched ball

Equipment: 3 balls, a bat, and a fence, backstop, or netting

Procedure: This drill is designed for paired players. One player tosses pitches while the other player bats. Position the batter so the ball is hit into a fence, net, or backstop. Position the pitcher about 10 ft away and at a 45° angle to the batter. This position will allow the pitcher to toss easy underhand pitches to the batter, who can hit the ball into the fence or net.

(1.6) Batting/Fielding Drill

Age: 9 years and up

Purpose: To develop batting skills and to help fielders react to hit balls

Equipment: Enough balls and bats to have batting practice and one complete set of bases

Procedure: Divide the team into batters and fielders. Have one batter and one "on-deck" batter. All other players are fielders. The coach or actual pitcher pitches 15 balls to each batter. The fielders should field the ball, throw to second base, to first base, and back to the pitcher. When a batter's turn is over, have him or her take a defensive position. The on-deck batter moves up to bat, and another fielder moves to the on-deck spot.

(1.7) Wrist Roller Drill

Age: 9 years and up

Purpose: To enhance bat control by strengthening the wrists

Equipment: Bats

Procedure: Have players get into a contact position and roll the bat forward and backward so that the bat touches each shoulder. Your players should use only their wrists and forearms to rotate the bat.

(1.8) Bunt Drill

Age: 9 years and up

Purpose: To develop the fundamentals of bunting

Equipment: A bat and ball for every two players

Procedure: Your players can work on bunting alone or with a partner. When alone, have them move from the batting stance to square position with an imaginary pitcher; then hold the bat in the proper bunting position and punch at an imaginary pitched ball.

With a partner, the players alternate tossing pitches and bunting. One player stands about 15 to 20 ft from the other player and tosses easy pitches. The bunter should (a) assume the proper batting stance, (b) turn and squarely face the partner, (c) hold the bat in the proper bunt position, and (d) bunt the ball on the ground. After 10 to 12 bunts, players switch positions.

Chapter 2: Baserunning

Introduction: Running the Bases

The success of your players' baserunning will depend upon both their physical abilities and mental awareness. They must run as quickly as possible under control, know how to slide, avoid other players, and respond to instructions from the base coaches. Such a combination of all-out effort, field awareness, and body control makes baserunning a crucial, but particularly difficult skill for beginning players. In this chapter the particular needs of young athletes for learning and for performing baserunning skills will be explained, along with the following topics:

- Leaving the batter's box
- Running past first base
- Rounding the bases
- Coaching the bases
- Leaving a base
- Sliding
- Baserunning drills

Leaving the Batter's Box

When a batter hits a pitched ball, he or she becomes a base runner and must run to first base. Teach your players to run out of the box as soon as they hit the ball. Young players tend to watch the ball after hitting it rather than immediately running for first base. The moments players spend watching a ball could be the difference between being safe or out. A good way to develop this skill is to practice the Leaving the Batter's Box Drill (2.1)

Even though your players may think they will be out on easy fly balls or other apparent easy outs, remind them that they are safe until the umpire calls them out, and that they should run through first base each time they hit a ball. If they develop the habit of running hard after each hit, they will have a better chance to beat any close plays.

How to Leave the Batter's Box

To leave the batter's box and run to first base, instruct your players to turn from the follow-through batting position and step toward first base, as shown in Figure 2-1. Some players may run the first few steps sideways, or they may criss-cross their legs. If this occurs, demonstrate how to direct the first step toward first base (see Figure 2-2). If they look, turn, and step toward first base, they will not run sideways or criss-cross their feet.

Fig. 2-1

Fig. 2-2

Coaching Points
for Leaving the Batter's Box

1. Run! Do not watch the ball.
2. Turn the head and step toward first base.

Running Past First Base

Explain that running to first base is an all-out sprint and that they can run past first base without being tagged out, as shown in Figure 2-3. Therefore, teach your base runners to run as fast

Fig. 2-3

as possible until they are beyond first base. A useful strategy is to tell them to not start slowing down until they have taken at least one step beyond the base.

Even though they can run past first base, your players can be called out if they interfere with balls thrown to first base or with players fielding the ball. A good way to prevent interference calls and still reach first base quickly is to run along the baseline in foul territory rather than in fair territory (see Figure 2-3).

Also, as shown in Figure 2-4, young players tend to leap onto first base, which is not as fast as a running step. To reinforce these points, have your players practice the Running Past First Base Drill (2.2) described at the end of the chapter.

Coaching Points
for Running Past First Base

1. Run as fast as possible.
2. Run past first base.
3. Step on the front side of first base.
4. Do not jump onto first base.

Rounding the Bases

Rounding First Base

When a ball has been hit to the outfield, runners may be able to run around first base and go to

Fig. 2-4

second base. Running around a base is fairly easy, if done correctly. Show your players how to run wide just before reaching first base; then show them how to angle toward the base, touching the inside corner of the bag as shown in Figure 2-5 and to run another two steps while listening (not looking) for instructions from the base coach. If the base coach calls out, "Go to second," the runner can proceed to second base; but if the base coach calls out, "Stop at first," the runner should return to first base. Use the Rounding First Base Drill (2.3) and the Running From Home Plate to First Base Drill (2.4) to practice running to and around first base.

Rounding Second and Third Base

Rounding second base and third base is similar to rounding first base (see Figure 2-6). The player swings wide as he or she approaches the base, then angles in and touches the inside corner of the base. To reinforce these points and to practice running around second and third base, use the Running the Bases Drill (2.5).

Remind your players that unlike running to first base, they can be tagged out if they run beyond second or third base. Base runners can keep from overrunning a base by sliding or by coming to a standing stop. Sliding, explained later in this chapter, is a good way to stop and avoid being tagged out.

Fig. 2-5

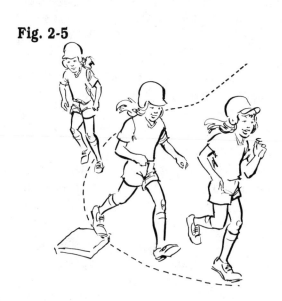

Fig. 2-6

Coaching Points for Rounding Bases

1. Look for and listen to the base coaches.
2. Swing outside of the base, angle toward the base, and touch the inside corner of the base.

Coaching the Bases

The importance of base coaches for an effective offense should not be overlooked. Coaching the bases is vital to a team's overall play and should be practiced just as your players practice baserunning. Both the first and third base coaches have two major responsibilities: (a) instructing the runner to remain at a base or advance to another, and (b) helping the runner leave the base. Many unnecessary errors are committed because runners are not told what to do, are told to do something they should not, or do not hear the base coach. Overcoming these problems is not easy. The job of base coaching needs to be practiced as often as your players practice their skills.

When coaching the bases, keep these following points in mind:

• Get the runner's attention by calling out loud and clear.

- Know what you want the runner to do and do not hesitate to call out instructions.
- Use short, easy-to-understand phrases rather than long sentences.
- Play it safe and avoid unnecessary risks.

First Base

The decision to stay at first base or run to second depends on where the ball is hit and on the ability of the runner; the result will either be an extra base or an out. Consequently, we suggest you play it safe and hold the runner to the base if there is any doubt about reaching the next base.

You can use any system for telling players to stay at first base or to run to second. Some suggested phrases for the first base coach that are short and easy for beginners to understand are "Run through," "Round first," and "Take second" (see Figure 2-7). Verbal communication at first base is so essential, because once the runner approaches first base, he or she should follow the instructions but not look for the base coach.

Coaching Second and Third Bases

When runners are on second base or are running past second to third, teach them to *look* and *listen* to the third base coach for instructions. Wave your arms and call out whether they should (a) stop at second or third base, or (b) run to home plate (refer to Figure 2-8).

Fig. 2-8

"Hold at second!"

Coaching Points for Base Coaching

1. Practice base coaching as your players practice baserunning.
2. Get the runner's attention and use short, clear statements.
3. Be cautious, don't take unnecessary risks.

Leaving A Base

Several running starts can be used to run from one base to another, including the track start, the rolling start, and the lead-off start. We suggest you teach young softball players one basic starting position (see Figure 2-9) and let them adjust this basic position to suit their own running style. During practices use the Base Start Drill (2.6) and the Leaving Bases Drill (2.7) which were expressly written to practice running from a base.

The basic starting position can be demonstrated quite easily. First, have your players face the next base; then show them how to get into a crouched position with one foot placed against the base and the other foot comfortably in front of the body as shown in Figure 2-10. Similar to a start in track, it is best to start by pushing off the base with the back foot, rather than stepping from the base and pushing off with the front foot.

Fig. 2-7

"Run through!"

Fig. 2-9

Fig. 2-10

As a base coach, you are responsible for telling the runner when to leave the base. According to softball rules, the runner cannot leave the base until the ball has been pitched or has left the pitching circle. (This is quite easy to determine.) However, there is another twist to leaving bases: caught fly balls. When a fly ball is hit, the runner is free to run to the next base; but if it is caught, the runner must return to that base and *tag up* before running. The best way to handle this situation is to teach your players to *lead off* far enough to run to the next base if the fly is not caught, but stay close enough to tag up if the fly is caught.

Sliding

Sliding is an effective way for base runners to reach a base and avoid a tag or to keep from running past the base. Actually, sliding is a controlled fall as the body glides over the top of the ground. It is a good idea not to teach sliding un-

til players are about 10 years old, or until they are skilled enough to slide without being hurt. Sliding is difficult to learn and can be dangerous for unskilled or very young players. Because sliding is a controlled fall, it is a difficult skill to teach in stages. However, sliding can be taught while running slowly and then progress to running faster.

The five basic slides are the *bent-leg* slide, the *stand-up* slide, the *decoy* slide, the *hook* slide, and the *head-first* slide. Do not teach all of these slides. Young players can easily injure themselves executing the head-first slide, stand-up slide, decoy slide, and hook slide. *Teach only the bent-leg slide* to your players and warn against the other slides. When the players are older, stronger, and more experienced, they will be able to learn and execute these other slides safely.

The Bent-Leg Slide

The bent-leg slide should start about 10 ft away from the base. To perform the bent-leg slide, show your base runners how to tuck one leg under the other leg, gently fall onto the bent leg, lean back, and sit down, as shown in Figure 2-11. Then to maintain balance, show your players how to hold the arms comfortably up and to the side. Players should not place their hands on the ground unless they lose control and begin to fall because the hands and arms could become injured if slid across the ground.

Coaching Points for Sliding

1. Begin to slide about 10 ft from the base.
2. Tuck one leg under the other.

Fig. 2-11

3. Lean back and sit down.

4. Keep arms held comfortably up off the ground.

Teaching Surfaces

Learning how to slide can be a great deal of fun for players if done in a safe environment. Water is a good teaching aid for presenting this skill. (Youngsters especially enjoy getting wet.) Players should be barefoot and wear either bathing suits or shorts and T-shirts.

Obtain long sheets of strong plastic (easily available as weatherproofing for windows); lay out these plastic sheets on grass fields which are free of ruts, rocks, or any other hazards, and then hose down the plastic. (This surface really encourages sliding.) Have your players run on grass up to the plastic sheet and slide; however, do not let players run on the plastic because they could slip, fall, and hurt themselves.

Watering down the grass provides a similar surface, but because the grass will not be as slippery as the plastic, players should wear socks, long pants, and long sleeved shirts to avoid abrasions.

Another option is to have players practice sliding on a properly prepared infield. The infield should have a sandy or loose dirt surface and be smooth and firm, but not hard. It is a good idea for players to wear socks, long-sleeved shirts, and pants to help prevent sliding burns.

Baserunning Drills

(2.1) Leaving the Batter's Box Drill

Age: 9 years and up

Equipment: Home plate and batter's box

Purpose: To train batters/base runners to focus their attention on first base and to run toward first base quickly

Procedure: All players line up in back of the backstop or a safe distance from home plate. One player at a time stands in the batter's box and swings at an imaginary pitch. As soon as the swing is completed, the player turns and runs about 10 steps toward first base. (Do not let them run all the way to first base.)

Help your players through this drill by giving them one or two short instructions; say "Look at first base" or "Step toward first," rather than talking your players through the entire drill.

(2.2) Running Past First Base Drill

Age: All

Purpose: To teach players to run past first base

Equipment: Bases (one base for each group practicing the drill)

Procedure: Set up the bases at regulation distance. Line up players at home plate. Have your players stand in the batter's box, simulate a swing, and run past first base. Encourage them to run at game speed.

(2.3) Rounding First Base Drill

Age: 9 and up

Purpose: To teach players how to run around first base

Equipment: Bases (enough for each group practicing the drill)

Procedure: Set up bases at regulation distances and place a mark about 15 ft before first base so your players know where to begin to turn toward second base. Have your players get into position in the batter's box, swing, and run to and round first base. Players initially run at a moderate speed, then gradually increase their running speed as they become better at running around first base.

(2.4) Running from Home Plate to First Base Drill

Age: All

Purpose: To teach players to listen and react to the first base coach

Equipment: Three first bases, three home plates, one bat per player

Procedure: Set up three sets of home plates and first bases at regulation distances, and line up your players at home plate. This set-up will let three players practice at the same time. The players swing a bat and run to first base. As the player approaches first base, the coach calls out, "Run past first" or "Round the base."

(2.5) Running the Bases Drill

Age: 9 years and up

Equipment: Infield bases

Purpose: To give players practice running bases

Procedure: Players start in the batter's box, simulate a swing, and run to first base. The coach at first base calls out, "Run through first base," "Take the turn," or "Run to second." After each runner has completed his or her turn, the next runner starts. Have base coaches at first and third bases direct your base runners. The third base coach directs runners reaching second base by calling, "Stay at second," "Round second," or "Run to third." Similar instructions are given when the runner reaches third base.

(2.6) Base Start Drill

Age: 9 years and up

Purpose: To practice running from one base to another base

Equipment: A complete infield set up with bases

Procedure: Set up an infield with bases and have one player act as the pitcher. Position base runners on first, second, and third bases. Have the base runners set up in the starting position and run from the base just as the pitcher releases the ball. Rotate your players around the bases. Have a new runner move to first base, and the runner on third base move to the end of the line.

(2.7) Leaving Bases Drill

Age: 9 years and up

Purpose: To practice leaving the base as fast as possible and returning to base for tag-ups

Equipment: One complete set of bases

Procedure: Position players on first base, second base, and third base. Be sure each player assumes the correct starting position. Call out, "Go" or "Run" to start the runner toward the next base. Call out, "Leave," "Tag up," or "Run" for leaving the base and tagging up after caught fly balls. Emphasize watching fly balls, listening to the base coach, and pushing off with the back foot. Rotate the runners around the bases. The runner on third base moves to the end of the line and a new runner moves to first base.

Part II:
Defensive Play

Defensive softball skills are much more specialized than are offensive skills. Hitting and baserunning are similar for all players regardless of whether they are first or sixth in the batting order. Defense is different because there are 9 players on the field at once and each player needs to learn the skills and responsibilities relative to his or her position.

Each chapter in this section is devoted to the various defensive aspects of softball. Separate chapters are included for (a) skills which all fielders need, (b) general infield and outfield skills, (c) infield and outfield skills specific to each position, (d) infield and outfield team play, and (e) pitching and catching.

Chapter 3: Defensive Fundamentals

Introduction: Defensive Skills

The physical skills needed to play defense vary according to the position played and the particular game situation. Conversely, each playing situation determines the type of skills needed to make a play. Moving quickly to the ball and throwing hard are skills using large muscles and do not require great precision. However, actually fielding or catching the ball and throwing accurately are more refined skills requiring greater precision; thus, beginning players may have difficulty performing these more accurate and precise skills.

We recommend you begin by teaching your players defensive fundamentals, and then progress to more advanced defensive concepts. If you follow this progression, your players will not only learn how to play defense, but will also understand the principles of defensive play.

To help your players begin learning to play defense, the following defensive topics are presented in this chapter:

- Selecting, caring for, and using the glove
- Throwing mechanics
- Catching the ball
- General defensive drills

The Glove

Selecting the Glove

Selecting a softball glove is important because it is the tool your players use to field and catch. Without the proper tool, defensive play will suffer. If you are able to talk to your players or their parents before they buy their gloves, point out two considerations: the size of the glove as compared to the size of the hand and the size of the glove's pocket.

The glove should be small enough to fit comfortably on a player's hand, and the pocket should be large. Furthermore, the glove should be easy for the player to control. For young softball players, a broken-in smaller glove will be much more useful than a larger glove. It is not a good idea for youngsters to play with an oversized glove in hopes of later growing into it (see Figure 3-1). Beginning players need a well-fitting glove from the outset in order to learn softball basics. Oversized gloves that they cannot control will be an ineffective tool and will hinder the development of defensive playing skills.

The first thing to decide is which hand wears the glove. Most people can control the glove better with the nondominant hand and can throw

Fig. 3-1

better with the dominant hand. Therefore, to select the hand which wears the glove, have your players hold up the throwing hand and have them place the glove on the other (nonthrowing) hand.

Caring for and Conditioning the Glove

Conditioning the glove will help your players control the glove and will improve their ability to field and to hold the ball. Conditioning is sometimes called *breaking in* the glove and will create a good pocket for the softball by making it more manageable. Explain the following break-in procedures to your players.

1. Rub some hot water into the center of the glove and work it in.
2. Place two softballs in the glove pocket and tie the glove around the balls as illustrated in Figure 3-2.

Fig. 3.2

3. Leave the glove tied overnight; repeat this process each evening until the glove has formed a good round pocket and is very flexible.
4. Use glove oil, saddle soap, or leather oil periodically. Rub the oil into the glove and let the oil soak into the glove overnight. However, be sure to rub off any excess oil before you use the glove! The glove will gradually become strong and flexible.

Using the Glove

The hand should fit into the glove with all five fingers so that it becomes an extension of the catching hand (see Figure 3-3). Keeping all five

Fig. 3-3

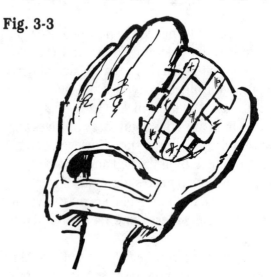

PROPER HAND PLACEMENT IN GLOVE

IMPROPER HAND PLACEMENT IN GLOVE

fingers in the glove helps control the ball as well as protect fingers. Demonstrate how the glove can be opened and closed as easily as moving the hand. Removing the index finger from the glove in order to increase the pocket size is not a good idea. This actually reduces control of the glove and increases the risk of injury to the exposed finger.

Throwing Mechanics

Because children grow up throwing rocks, balls, and flying discs, knowing how to throw is sometimes taken for granted. However, learning how to throw a softball *accurately* takes much practice. The following discussion focuses on teaching your players the *overhand* throw. (We suggest you wait until your players know how to throw overhand well before you teach the *sidearm* throw.)

Two drills are presented at the end of this chapter to help your players practice throwing mechanics. The Flick the Ball Drill (3.1) focuses on the arm and wrist action, and the Throwing Action Drill (3.2) focuses on stepping into the throw and swinging the throwing arm.

The Grip

How a player grips the ball will greatly affect how it is thrown; many throwing errors will be prevented if your players first know how to grip the ball properly. Explain that the ball should rest only on the fingers and not in the palm (see Figure 3-4), with the thumb on the bottom of the ball and the other four fingers spread on the top. If the ball is held in the palm of the hand, it will be difficult to control. To help your players develop a firm but flexible throwing grip, have them practice the Ball Grip Drill (3.4).

How to Throw

Although the mechanics of throwing can be very complex, they can and should be presented simply to beginning players. Throwing mechanics have been divided into these four easy-to-understand phases: the ready position, shifting onto the back foot, stepping toward the target and throwing the ball, and the follow-through.

Phase 1: Getting in the Ready Position
Have your players face the target squarely with the body evenly balanced on both feet and with a proper but comfortable grip, and focus their eyes on the target, as shown in Figure 3-5. The importance of this preparation is to begin the throw, balanced and with the body and ball under control.

Phase 2: Shifting
The body weight is simply shifted onto the throwing side (push-off) leg as the front leg is lifted off the ground. At the same time, the throwing arm swings back with the wrist cocked (see Figure 3-6).

Fig. 3-4

Fig. 3-5

Fig. 3-6

Phase 3: Throwing the Ball

The body weight should now shift onto the front leg as the back leg pushes forward. With this push, the front leg strides out and lands slightly bent. This will help a player maintain balance and smoothly transfer energy from the push-off leg toward the target. You can really help a player by watching this phase carefully. If a player's stride is too long or too short, as shown in Figure 3-7, the throw will be inaccurate, and you will need to adjust the stride.

After striding and planting the front foot, the upper body is able to turn toward the target. This helps pull the throwing arm around the body toward the target. After the arm moves forward, the wrist snaps to send the ball flying, as shown in Figure 3-8.

Phase 4: Following Through

The follow-through is actually the result of a good throw, because once the ball is released, a player can no longer affect the throw; therefore, a good throw will have a good follow-through. Demon-

Fig. 3-7

LONG   SHORT   PROPER
                             LENGTH

Fig. 3-8

strate that in the follow-through, the throwing arm is extended and continues across the body. The leg used to push off (back leg) steps through and lands ahead of the glove-side foot (see Figure 3-9).

Coaching Points for the Throw

1. Leg work is important because most of the power for the throw comes from the legs. To demonstrate, have your players try to throw without using the legs.
2. Concentrate upon the target at all times, even during the follow-through.
3. The shoulders should remain level until the follow-through. If the shoulders are dipped up or down, the throw will be off target.
4. Snapping the wrist will put a backward spin on the ball; this indicates a good release and helps the ball travel in a straight line.

Quickness, Accuracy, and Speed

You will want your players to make quick, accurate, and fast throws, but the quicker the ball

Fig. 3-9

is released and the faster the ball is thrown, the more difficult it is to control. Because of this, it is more important to have beginning players first develop accuracy by throwing at moderate speeds, then gradually increase the speed of the throws, maintaining accuracy.

Teaching Progression for Throwing

Remember, your players will learn throwing best if they are taught in a purposeful progression. The following teaching progression has been designed to help you teach throwing to your players effectively.

1. Introduce the grip.
2. Explain and demonstrate the starting position.
3. Teach players to shift the weight onto the back foot and prepare to throw.
4. Demonstrate and explain how to step toward the target and release the ball.
5. Teach players not to stop after the ball is released but to always follow through.
6. *Emphasize control.* Increase the speed of the throw while maintaining accuracy.

Catching

Catching a softball involves excellent hand-eye coordination and much practice. Thrown balls travel a long distance and can often fool the fielder by changing direction and by giving the illusion of appearing to move faster as they approach. The Warm-up Catching and Throwing Drill (3.4) is very useful for developing the skills needed to catch a softball.

Instructing Players to Catch

• Give the thrower a target by holding out the glove. This will help the thrower aim the ball (see Figure 3-10).
• Move the body in line with the ball as illustrated in Figure 3-11. Demonstrate how to step toward and away from the ball, and how to step sideways using a sidestep motion.
• Watch the ball. Tell your players to look at the ball all the way from the thrower's hand into the glove.

Fig. 3-10

PROVIDE A GOOD TARGET

Fig. 3-11

MOVE TO THE BALL

• Catch the ball in the pocket of the glove, not in the fingers. Explain that the glove pocket is made to hold the ball while the fingers are made to give players control of the glove.
• Trap the ball with the throwing hand as shown in Figure 3-12. Let your players know that trapping the ball will help secure the catch and will allow them to grip and throw the ball more quickly.
• Absorb the impact of the throw as in Figure 3-13 by allowing the glove to move toward the body after the catch. This is called *cushioning* the ball.

Your players will need to adjust the glove position depending upon the location of the throw. By using the guidelines listed below and the illustrated Figures 3-14 to 3-17, instruct your

Fig. 3-12

CATCH AND TRAP BALL

Fig. 3-13

CUSHION THE BALL

Fig. 3-14

CATCHING ABOVE THE WAIST

players on the following body and glove adjustments:

1. If the ball is above the waist, have the fingers of the glove point up.
2. If the ball is below the waist, have the fingers of the glove point down.

Fig. 3-15

CATCHING BELOW THE WAIST

Fig. 3-16

CATCHING TO THE THROWING SIDE

Fig. 3-17

CATCHING TO THE GLOVE SIDE

3. If the ball is on the throwing side of the body, have the back of the glove face the body and the thumb face down.
4. If the ball is on the glove side of the body, instruct your players to hold the glove with the thumb up and the fingers pointing out.

Teaching Progression for Catching

1. Instruct your players on the proper use of the glove.
2. Stress the importance of watching the throw.
3. Show your players how to move to the ball by stepping forward, backward, or to the side.
4. Explain that the ball should be caught in the pocket of the glove and trapped with the throwing hand.
5. Demonstrate how to cushion the catch by moving the glove toward the body.

General Defensive Drills

(3.1) Flick the Ball Drill

Age: 9 years and up

Purpose: To develop throwing skills by emphasizing strong wrist action and proper ball spin

Equipment: One ball for every two players, gloves

Procedure: Players work in pairs. Partners stand only 10-12 ft apart and face one another. Players flick the ball back and forth, using only the wrist and aiming at the chest. To isolate the wrist action from the arm motion, have the players bend and place their elbow in the palm of their other hand.

Fig. 3-18

(3.2) Throwing Action Drill

Age: 9 years and up

Purpose: To help young players develop the proper arm throwing motion

Equipment: One ball for each player

Procedure: Have your players work individually. This drill is divided into two phases. In the first phase, have players grip the ball properly. Then, players should practice getting into the ready position and shift their feet, arms, and weight to prepare for the throw. In the second phase, have players get set by shifting their feet, arms, and weight (end of Phase I) and complete the throwing motion by striding forward, pushing off the back leg, and swinging the throwing arm forward.

(3.3) Ball Grip Drill

Age: 9 years and up

Purpose: To develop coordination of fingers and wrist for proper grip of ball, and to develop strength in the fingers and forearm

Equipment: One ball for every two players

Procedure: Have players pair up. One player grips the ball with a proper throwing grip. The partner tries to remove the ball by moving it up and down and to the side. The player holding the ball should keep a flexible wrist and allow the hand to move up and down while maintaining a firm grip on the ball. The partner who is pulling on the ball should not jerk the ball, but should keep an even pull on the ball. After 30 seconds, players switch roles; this allows each player to rest his or her hand before the next repetition. Repeat this two to three times.

(3.4) Warm-up Catching and Throwing Drill

Age: All

Purpose: To loosen and warm up players prior to throwing hard

Equipment: One ball for every two players, gloves

Procedure: Players pair up and throw to each other from relatively short distances. Players gradually increase the speed and distance they throw, but always throw comfortably, never hard.

Contest: Have players line up facing each other about 15 ft apart. Each time a pair successfully completes two throws apiece, they can take one step back; but each time a ball is misthrown and not caught, they must take one step toward each other.

Chapter 4: Fielding and Throwing Fundamentals

Introduction: The Importance of Judgment Skills

After your players have learned the fundamentals of throwing and catching, they will be ready to learn the fundamentals of fielding and throwing in game situations; they will learn to field balls hit on the ground and in the air and to catch balls thrown from another part of the field while staying close to a base. Unless these fielding and throwing fundamentals specific to game situations are properly taught, your players will have difficulty playing team defense.

These skills involve the ability to visually judge the speed and distance of a hit or thrown ball. Thus, your players must also learn how to react to the ball: Should they charge the ball or back up? Move to the right or left? Hold the glove up, down, or to the side? The abilities of visual judgment and movement reactions are not easy for beginning players to learn. As their coach, you will need to be patient and encourage them to develop these abilities. Keep this in mind as you teach your players the following information for fielding and throwing in game situations:

- The principal rule of fielding
- Developing good fielding and throwing habits
- Playing the ball and throwing

- The ready position
- Moving to the ball
- Taking in ground balls
- Taking in fly balls
- Throwing the ball
- Tagging runners out
- Fielding and throwing drills

The Principal Rule of Fielding

Before you teach these defensive skills, be sure your players understand the principal rule of fielding which is, *keep the ball in front*. By keeping the ball in front of the body, your players will eliminate many errors caused by reaching out to the side and not moving to the ball. This rule also directs the positioning of your outfielders, preventing fly balls from being hit beyond them.

Developing Good Fielding and Throwing Habits

The development of fielding and throwing fundamentals is extremely important for proficient game play now and enjoyment of the game in the future. The more your players practice to develop correct habits, the better they will play today and in the future.

Tell your players to think of habits as ways people act automatically without concentrating on what they are doing. For example, the way they eat and scratch their head are considered habits. Habits are learned by repeating an action so many times that you do not consciously decide what to do, you just act. You can help your beginning players develop correct playing habits by following the guidelines explained in the ACEP Level 1 book *Coaching Young Athletes* and by structuring practices in such a way that players repeatedly perform these fundamentals. As you do this, provide encouragement and correct mistakes positively through demonstrations and explanations.

Playing the Ball and Throwing

Fielding can be divided into two main categories: *playing the ball* and *throwing*. Explain that playing the ball means reacting to and catching a hit or thrown ball; throwing involves moving the ball from one part of the field to another in order to complete defensive plays.

In addition to teaching the *how's* of fielding and throwing, you will also need to teach the *why's* and *where's*, or playing strategy. For example, after the ball is taken in, where should it be thrown, and why should the players throw there? Many strategy factors such as the speed of the runners, their position on base, the number of outs, and the score of the game will determine where the ball is played. These playing strategy factors are discussed in the section on playing strategy in chapter 7.

The Ready Position

Once the game begins, every player must be ready to perform the responsibilities of his or her position. But, if the player is not in a comfortable ready position, he or she will not be able to move easily or play well. The best ready position depends upon the player. A ready position that is comfortable for one player may not be good for another. Therefore, as you teach the ready position, help each player find the style that is both comfortable and effective for him or her.

The Ready Position Stance

The ready position is quite simple. Players stand with the feet about hip-width apart, with the knees bent and the body weight over the balls of the feet as illustrated in Figure 4-1. Gloves should be open wide and held comfortably inside the legs. Because ground balls can change direction or bounce unexpectedly, watching the ball all the way into the glove is very important. The Fielding Position Drill (4.1) is a good drill for practicing the fielding ready position and for preparing to move to the ball.

Coaching Points for Ready Position

1. Stand with the feet about hip-width apart for a good base of support.
2. To move quickly in every direction, keep the knees bent.
3. For quick movement, keep the weight on the balls of the feet. Standing flat-footed slows movement to the ball.
4. Be sure the hands are held low between the legs with the glove open wide.

Moving to the Ball

Once the ready position is learned, you can teach your players how to react and move to the ball.

Fig. 4-1

It is important they learn to react to the ball as soon as it is hit. If they wait until the ball is halfway down the infield, they will not be able to reach it in time to make a play.

Determining Movement Direction

Your fielders can reach the ball quickly by determining the direction of the ball and moving toward it; most often players need to move forward or backward, and then change direction. Demonstrate how to move forward by stepping out of the starting position, running forward, and keeping the arms low to the field, as shown in Figure 4-2.

The Side Step

The *side step* is one of the two methods used to move from side to side. Use the side step for moving short distances by shuffling the feet from side to side, but not crossing them. The advantage of the side step is in keeping a balanced stance while moving to the ball (see Figure 4-3).

The Crossover Step

The second method, the *crossover step*, il-

Fig. 4-2

Fig. 4-3

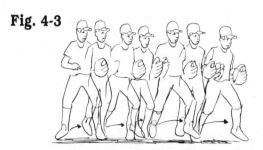

lustrated in Figure 4-4, should be used when a player needs to turn and run quickly for longer distances. To teach the crossover step, have each player step across the body with one foot while the body pivots around the other foot which remains planted. After the foot has crossed over, the player is in position to run in that direction.

Moving Backward

When your players need to move backward, they can simply step backward or use the crossover step to turn to the side and then run back. For moving short distances, stepping back is more effective than crossing over and running back. For example, if a ball is popped up to the second baseman, he or she has plenty of time to watch the ball while taking a few steps backward.

The crossover step should be used to run a long distance quickly. For example, if the ball is hit over the head of the second baseman and toward the shallow outfield, the second baseman should use the crossover step to turn and run to the outfield.

Coaching Points for Moving to the Ball

1. Move to the ball when it is hit. Waiting for the ball will waste time and could prevent the team from making an out.

Fig. 4-4

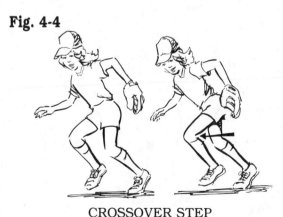

CROSSOVER STEP

2. Watch the ball all the way into the glove.
3. Use the side step or crossover step to move sideways, and the crossover step or back step to move backwards.

Taking In Ground Balls

The next step in learning to field is called *taking in* the ball and involves getting the ball up from the ground and into the glove. Have your players bend down with the legs (keeping the back straight) and reach out the glove to meet the ball (see Figure 4-5). Emphasize that trapping the ball with the throwing hand is as important as fielding a thrown ball. Practicing the Fielding Ground Balls Drill (4.2) and the Charge the Ball Drill (4.3) will reinforce these points and help your players develop the ability to field ground balls.

Cushioning the Ball

When taking in a ball, encourage your players to keep the wrists firm yet flexible in order to *cushion* the ball. With a flexible wrist, the force of the ball should softly punch back the glove and prevent the ball from popping out.

Fielding Short Hops

Many ground balls will *short hop* or bounce from the ground directly in front of the fielder. These are the real tricky grounders that are difficult to field. There is no guaranteed method for fielding short hops, but it will help if your fielders have

Fig. 4-5

FIELDING POSITION

relaxed arms and hold the glove open and out in front of the body. Short hops can bounce wildly and your players should be ready to rise up or down or move the glove quickly.

Coaching Points for Fielding Ground Balls

1. Get into position before the ball is taken in. Once again, emphasize the importance of being prepared to field the ball.
2. Watch the ball.
3. Trap the ball.
4. Cushion the ball.

Teaching Progression for Fielding Ground Balls

1. Teach players the ready position.
2. Teach players how to move forward, backward, and to the side.
3. Teach players how to take in and trap ground balls.
4. Progress from easy to more difficult ground balls by slowly rolling grounders thrown from short distances, gradually increasing the speed and distance.

Taking In Fly Balls

Explain to your players that when a ground ball is fielded, the runner must be thrown out, but if a fly ball is caught, the runner is *automatically* out. The two basic glove positions for taking in fly balls are illustrated in Figure 4-6. For fly balls caught above the chest, show your players how to hold the glove above the shoulders with the fingers pointing upward. For fly balls caught below the chest, use the *basket catch* by holding the glove about waist height with the pocket facing upward.

Trapping Fly Balls

As with fielding ground balls, remind your fielders to trap the ball. But be careful how you teach this; trapping fly balls is different from trapping ground balls. We suggest that the free

Fig. 4-6

FLY BALL ABOVE CHEST

FLY BALL BELOW CHEST

hand be held in back to first support the glove and cushion the ball, and then to close the glove around the ball, as shown in Figure 4-7.

Calling for Fly Balls

Because fly balls travel across several infield positions, more than one fielder may try for the catch. Also, if a player is watching the ball, he or she may not see other players who are also trying to field the fly ball. You can prevent many unnecessary collisions by teaching your players to yell "Mine!" or "I have it!" when the fly ball is at its highest point (peak) as shown in Figure 4-8, so the player with the best position can watch the ball drop and make the catch.

Fig. 4-7

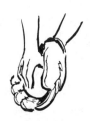

Fig. 4-8

Judging Fly Balls

Beginning players may find fielding fly balls difficult because of the speed of the ball and the distance it travels. Several different indicators will help your players determine how well a fly ball is hit. The first indicator is the sound of the bat contacting the ball. The stronger and the more solid the sound, the better the hit. The second indicator for judging fly balls is the speed of the ball as it leaves the bat. The faster the ball leaves the bat, the better the hit and the farther it will travel. The third indicator for judging fly balls is the angle of the ball; the steeper the angle, the higher the ball will fly (see Figure 4-9). If a ball leaves the bat fast and has a moderate angle, it will travel farther than a ball that is hit fast and has a steep or low angle.

Unfortunately, there is no easy method for teaching how to determine what a solid hit sounds like (especially if a metal bat is used), or to teach the speed of a ball leaving the bat, or the distance a ball will travel. The best teacher for these skills will be the experience of practicing

Fig. 4-9

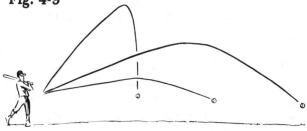

the Judging Fly Balls Drill (4.4) and the other drills listed in chapter 6, "Playing the Outfield."

Coaching Points for Taking In Fly Balls

1. Watch the ball.
2. Stand up from the ready position.
3. Move sideways and backwards, using the side step or crossover step, or back step.
4. Call for the ball when it is at its highest point.
5. When catching fly balls above the chest, hold the glove facing up and above the chest. When catching fly balls below the chest, hold the glove about waist height with the open pocket facing the ball.
6. Trap the ball by placing the free hand behind the glove and closing the glove around the ball.

Teaching Progression for Fielding Fly Balls

1. Teach the ready position.
2. Teach how to move to the ball.
3. Instruct your players to call for fly balls.
4. Teach how to trap fly balls.
5. Progress from easy to more difficult fly balls. Begin with easy lobs from short distances. Gradually increase the distance and height of the fly balls.

Throwing the Ball

Once a ball is fielded, it should be thrown to the appropriate base or player as quickly and accurately as possible. To get extra power on the throw and maintain accuracy, teach your players the three phases of the *skip and throw*, and practice the Step and Throw Drill (4.5), the Throw and Step Back Drill (4.6), and the Throwing for Points Drill (4.7).

The Skip

The first phase of the skip and throw is a short skip, as shown in Figure 4-10, which provides extra momentum and power. Show your players how to skip by taking a short hop on the back

Fig. 4-10

(push-off) foot while the front foot moves forward and the arms are drawn back.

The Throwing Motion

This second phase involves the entire body, not just the arms. After skipping, the back foot pushes the body forward and the front leg steps directly toward the target. This push and forward step provides the power to whip the arm around and throw the ball (see Figure 4-11).

The Follow-Through

Remind your players that the follow-through is the result of a good throw. In a proper follow-through, the body pivots around the front foot while the throwing hand continues to swing across the body (see Figure 4-12).

Coaching Points for Throwing the Ball

1. Grip the ball in the glove.

Fig. 4-11

Fig. 4-12

Fig. 4-13

2. Skip on the back foot, push off, and step toward the target.
3. Focus on the target and swing the throwing arm forward.
4. Follow-through.

Teaching Progression for Throwing the Ball

1. Teach the skip. Emphasize a short, low skip rather than a long, high skip.
2. Teach the step and throw motion. Stress the coordination of the legs, arms, and body.
3. Teach the follow-through, which is the result of a good throw.
4. Combine the skip, step, and throw. Emphasize smooth and coordinated movements and an accurate throw.
5. Gradually progress from throwing easy, over short distances, to throwing over longer distances.

Fig. 4-14

Fig. 4-15

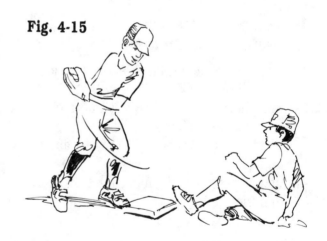

Tagging Runners Out

Now that your players know how to catch and field balls, they need to learn how to tag out base runners. This is an important fielding duty; it is also a situation where both the fielder and runner could be injured, so safety should be stressed. Demonstrate how to tag out base runners by studying the position and techniques shown in Figures 4-13 to 4-15 and explain the following points to your players:

1. Get into position behind and to the side of the base.

2. Catch the ball off to the side of the base.
3. Lay the glove down between the base and the runner.
4. Move the glove away after the runner has been tagged out.

The first priority of every fielder is to stop the ball, so if the throw is not on target, teach your players to move away from the base and catch the ball. Regardless of whether the runner is or is not tagged out, the ball must be caught, or the runner will definitely be safe and will probably advance to another base (see Figure 4-16).

Fig. 4-16

Coaching Points for Tagging the Runner

1. Position your fielders behind and to the side of the base.
2. Catch and hold onto the ball.
3. Lay the glove down between the base and the runner.
4. Move away from the runner.

Teaching Progression for Tagging the Runner

1. Teach how to stand behind and to the side of the base.
2. Teach how to move to the ball and catch the throw before reaching the base.
3. Lay the glove down between the base and the runner.
4. After the tag is made, move the glove away from the runner.

Fielding and Throwing Drills

The following drills have been designed to help your players learn the skills essential to softball defense. We recommend you select the drills which you feel will best help your players develop their softball skills, and modify the drills to meet the age and ability levels of your players.

(4.1) Fielding Position Drill

Age: 9 years and up

Purpose: To teach and refine the fielding ready position

Equipment: None

Procedure: Divide players among coaches (8 to 10 per coach). Instruct and demonstrate the fielding ready position and have your players line up in a semicircle. Call out, "Set," "Down," or "Up." On each command, the players should get set to field, bend their legs, and get down (as if taking in a ball), or straighten their legs and rise up to move quickly. Be sure to watch for poor mechanics and give positive, meaningful feedback to correct the skill.

(4.2) Fielding Ground Balls Drill

Age: 9 years and up

Purpose: To teach and refine the skill of fielding ground balls

Equipment: One ball for every two players, gloves

Procedure: Pair up players. Position players facing each other, a moderate distance apart. Start with players rolling easy ground balls to each other. Older and more skilled players can stand farther apart and throw ground balls harder.

(4.3) Charge The Ball Drill

Age: 9 years and up

Purpose: To develop aggressive movement to a ground ball and to develop proper fielding fundamentals

Equipment: Several balls, gloves

Procedure: If there is more than one coach, divide the team into two groups of 6 to 8 players. The players from each group practice with one coach. Have your players form two lines and face each other, 30 to 40 ft apart. Be sure your players are far enough apart to avoid interfering with each other. Have the players in the first line throw easy grounders to their partners. Instruct your fielding players to charge the ball rather than wait for the ball. Alternate fielders and throwers after 10 throws.

(4.4) Judging Fly Balls Drill

Age: 9 years and up

Purpose: To develop the visual judgment needed for responding to and catching fly balls

Equipment: Balls, gloves

Procedure: Divide your players among your assistant coaches. Have your players stand facing you from about 20 ft away. Throw each player relatively easy fly balls. Vary the height, arc, and speed of the balls you throw. As your players become more experienced and are able to catch these fly balls, move them farther from you and increase the difficulty of the fly balls. You should eventually progress to conducting this drill batting balls from the same distances as in actual games.

(4.5) Step and Throw Drill

Age: 9 years and up

Purpose: To practice the skip and throw

Equipment: One ball for every two players

Procedure: Pair up your players and position them apart a moderate distance. Have each player throw using the skip and throw. The skip should be low and short, and the player should step into the throw. This drill can also be modified to practice throwing after fielding a ground ball or fly ball.

(4.6) Throw and Step Back Drill

Age: 9 years and up

Purpose: To help players practice and refine throwing skills

Equipment: One ball for every two players, gloves

Procedure: Pair up players. Have partners stand reasonably close to each other. Players throw the ball back and forth. Each time the ball is successfully thrown and caught, the player who threw the ball takes a step back. When the ball is not caught, the player takes a step forward. This drill can also be used as a competition-type drill between team members.

(4.7) Throwing for Points Drill

Age: 9 years and up

Purpose: To develop the ability to focus on a specific spot before throwing and to throw to that spot accurately

Equipment: One ball for every two players, gloves

Procedure: Players work in pairs. Have players stand 30-40 ft apart and face one another. Players earn points by throwing to specific spots on the partner's body. Scoring: chest = 5 points; hips = 3 points; arms and legs = 1 point; head = 1 point; away from the body—subtract 1 point from the player's score. Have players hold the ball where they catch it so their partner can evaluate and correct the next throw. Suggested winning score is 50 points.

Chapter 5: Positional Infield Skills

Introduction: Infield Playing Areas

Because softball is such a popular game, many beginning players know some of the basics, such as where the bases are located and where the pitcher and catcher stand. However, before they can practice team defensive plays, they must learn the coverage areas and the responsibilities for the following six infield positions presented in this chapter:

- First baseman
- Second baseman
- Shortstop
- Third baseman
- Pitcher
- Catcher

Teaching positional responsibilities is important for two other reasons. First, if your fielders stray outside of the positional areas or do not fulfill the duties of their position, overall team defense will suffer. Studying this chapter carefully and teaching your players their responsibilities will greatly contribute to an effective team defense. The Infield Teamwork Drill (5.1), the Backing-Up Drill (5.2), and the Individual Position Drill (5.3) will give your players the experience of playing infield positions.

Second, we highly recommend that all beginning softball players learn several different positions (see Figure 5-1). Beginning softball players should not specialize at one position too soon. Let each player experience several positions, and then based on expressed preference, players can specialize as they mature.

The First Baseman

The first baseman's coverage area is not particularly large. It extends from midway between home plate and first base and over to about halfway between first and second base (see Figure 5-2). The important feature of this position is not the coverage area but rather to prevent runners from reaching the base safely. If a runner can be thrown out before reaching first base, a scoring opportunity is eliminated and the entire team can concentrate only on the next batter, rather than on the batter and a base runner.

Fig. 5-1

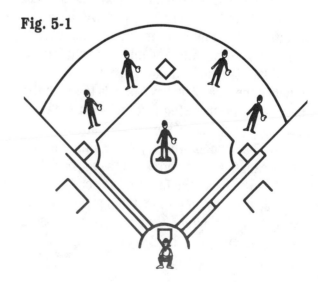

Fig. 5-2

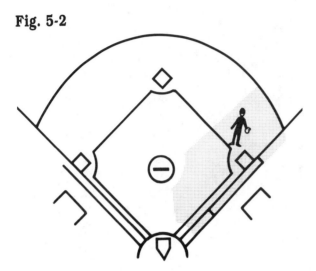

To field this area, position your first baseman a few steps toward second base and slightly behind first base. From this position, the first baseman can perform the following duties quickly and easily:

- Catching and fielding balls hit to the first base area
- Making force-outs by touching first base or throwing to other fielders covering first base
- Throwing to second base for force-outs
- Cutting off plays at home plate
- Relaying throws from right field
- Backing up second base

Plays at First Base

Beginning players need to be taught how to make force-outs at first base. Begin by explaining what a force-out is (chapter 11 of the Softball Planning Guide), and then emphasize these two points: (a) force-outs are more common at first base than are tag-outs; and (b) a force-out is good if the ball is caught and any part of the body touches the base. The key, then, is to touch the base with the throwing foot and to stretch out several feet to catch the ball as illustrated in Figure 5-3. Explain that by stretching out, the ball is caught sooner and as long as the back foot touches the base, the force-out is good.

While this position is great for force-outs, it is not good for moving after poorly thrown balls. Teach your players to be alert and to know where the throw is going before they stretch out for the

Fig. 5-3

catch. Remember, the first baseman's main priority is to catch the ball, even if it means leaving the base.

Coaching Points for Plays at First Base

1. Touch the inside of first base.
2. Reach out to catch the ball.
3. Leave first base to catch poor throws.

Throwing to First Base

When the first baseman fields a hit ball and cannot touch first base before the runner, the second baseman or pitcher must cover first base. By tossing the ball underhand to other fielders covering first base (see Figure 5-4), the ball will reach the base in time to make the out and will be easier to catch than an overhand throw.

Cutting Off Throws to Home Plate

The first baseman must be ready to move in front of home plate to cut off relay throws (see Figure 5-5). Line up the first baseman about 15 ft in front of home plate. Also, emphasize listening for

Fig. 5-4

Fig. 5-5

FIRST BASEMEN CUT OFF THROWS TO HOME PLATE

the catcher calling out "cut off," or "come through."

The Second Baseman

The second baseman covers a large area from about midway between first and second base, over to second base, and from behind the pitcher's area to the shallow portion of right and center fields (see Figure 5-6). Even though this is a lot of ground to cover, the second baseman is close to the two bases where most plays will be made: first base and second base. This means that the second baseman will not make many long throws, can play from a relatively deep position, and can perform the following duties:

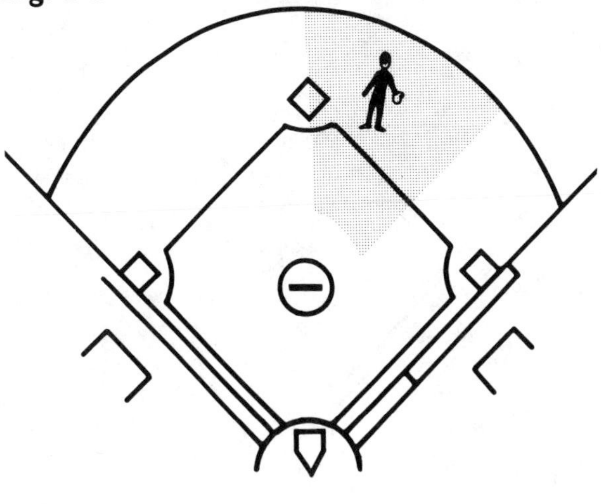

- Fielding balls hit to the coverage area
- Throwing to second and first base for force-outs
- Tagging out runners moving from first to second base
- Making force-outs and tag-outs at second base
- Covering first base on bunts and whenever the first baseman fields the ball
- Relaying throws from the outfield to the infield
- Backing up second base when the shortstop is making the play

The Shortstop

The shortstop has a wide area to cover: from second base almost to third base and to the shallow outfield. The best starting position for shortstop (see Figure 5-7) is about halfway between third base and second base; however, the ability of each player will determine his or her exact position. Because the shortstop has a large area to cover and because throws to first base are long, those players who are more mobile and who can throw far will be able to play from a deeper position; those players who are less mobile or who cannot throw as far will need to play a bit more shallow. Keep these points in mind as you teach your players the following responsibilities for the shortstop:

- Fielding all balls hit to the coverage area

Fig. 5-6

Fig. 5-7

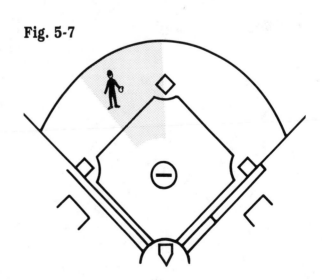

- Throwing to second and first base for force-outs
- Relaying and cutting off throws from the outfield
- Covering second base on bunt attempts or when balls are hit to the second baseman
- Backing up second base when the second baseman is making the play

The Third Baseman

The third baseman covers the infield area from about halfway down the third baseline over to the shortstop position and back to the shallow part of left field (see Figure 5-8). This is not a large area to cover, but because it is far away from first and second base, the third baseman needs to have a good throwing arm. Most beginning players bat right-handed and tend to hit the ball to the shortstop or third base area, so it is very important to teach the third baseman to guard the third base foul line. If a ball is hit down the line and past third base, it will roll a long way before it is fielded and the batter will probably run to second base.

A good playing position for the third baseman is to be a few steps from the foul line and slightly behind third base. From this position the third baseman can guard the line and perform the following duties:

- Throwing to first base for force-outs
- Making plays at third base
- Relaying and cutting off throws from the outfield
- Covering bunts hit to the third base side of the infield
- Backing up the shortstop

The Pitcher

A common misconception about pitching is that the pitcher has few fielding responsibilities. This is not true: You will need to stress that the pitching position is not just for throwing the ball to the batter. The pitcher is another defensive player and has the following fielding duties:

- Backing up plays at home plate
- Covering first base when the first baseman is fielding a ball
- Backing up second and third base on throws from the outfield
- Fielding bunts
- Backing up throws to home plate

The defensive coverage area for pitchers extends from the back and sides of the pitching circle up to the home plate area (see Figure 5-9). In fact, the pitching follow-through places the pitcher in the front of the pitching circle close to the batter. This means pitchers must be prepared to react quickly to field balls after completing the pitch.

Fig. 5-8

Fig. 5-9

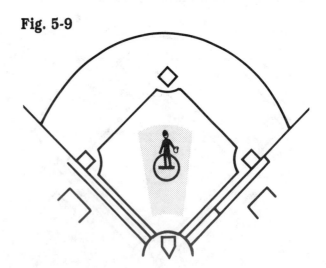

The pitcher must also back up home plate. When backing up home plate, position your pitchers about 10 ft in back of the plate, in line with the throw. From this position, the pitcher can still move in to home plate when throws get by the catcher.

The Catcher

Just as pitchers do more than pitch, catchers must do much more than catch pitches. The catcher's fielding area, illustrated in Figure 5-10, extends behind the plate to the backstop, along the first and third baselines, and in front of the plate about halfway to the pitcher's circle. In addition to catching pitches, catchers have the following duties:

- Protecting the plate by tagging out runners who attempt to score
- Fielding balls hit near or behind home plate
- Throwing to first, second, and third bases for tag-outs
- Backing up first base
- Fielding bunts

Catching Pop-Ups

Pop-ups hit near and in back of home plate present unusual problems for catchers. Other fielders will not be in position to help make the

Fig. 5-10

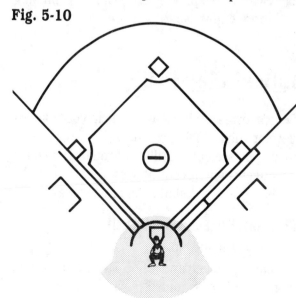

catch, and the catching equipment makes locating, moving to, and fielding the ball difficult. Show your catchers how to turn toward the location of the pitch, how to remove the facemask, and how to throw the mask away from the play, as shown in Figure 5-11. These skills can be practiced by performing the Pop-Ups for Catchers Drill (5.4).

Pop-ups hit close to the backstop are also difficult for young catchers. Show your players how to turn and face the backstop, as illustrated in Figure 5-12, rather than keeping the back to the backstop. As with your other fielders, instruct your catchers to always catch the ball with two hands.

Tagging Out Runners at Home Plate

Tagging out runners at home plate is an important skill for the catchers and is the last chance they have to prevent a run from scoring. They must also be careful, because according to the rules, the catcher may not interfere with the runner by blocking the plate unless the catcher is

Fig. 5-11

Fig. 5-12

tagging out that runner. Interfering with the runner could result in the umpire awarding the runner home plate.

Demonstrate the proper position for tag-outs at home plate, as in Figure 5-13, by positioning your players in front of and to the third-base side of home plate. From this position, they can catch the ball and make the tag without interfering with the runner. After your players understand how to position themselves and make the tag, have them practice the Tag Plays at Home Drill (5.5).

Backing Up First Base

Another important responsibility of the catcher is backing up first base. Because the catcher is positioned behind the batter, he or she is in an excellent position to see where the ball is hit, to follow the batter to first base, and to recover balls that get by the first baseman (see Figure 5-14).

Fig. 5-13

Fig. 5-14

CATCHERS BACK UP FIRST BASE

Running back and forth between home plate and first base is also a good way to wear out your players and eliminate volunteers for the catching position. We suggest you teach backing up first base to those players who are mature enough to handle this physical activity and also to use more than one catcher each game.

Dropped Third Strikes

Tell your players that in fast-pitch softball, there is an unusual play called *running on a dropped third strike*. Here is how it works: When no runner is on first base with less than two outs, and a third strike pitch is dropped (with two outs, first base can be occupied), the batter can run to first base. But, if the catcher can tag the batter or throw to first base before he or she touches the base, the runner is out. The best way to handle a dropped third strike is for you to call out, "Dropped third strike" and let the catcher tag the runner or throw the ball. A good drill to practice throwing to first base on dropped third strikes is the Throwing From the Stance Drill (5.6).

Fortunately, these plays do not happen regularly. Several of the rule modifications found in chapter 12 of the Softball Planning Guide eliminate the possibility of dropped third strike plays for players who may not be skilled or experienced enough to make these plays. We suggest you read and consider using these modifications. They can make playing softball less confusing and more enjoyable.

Infield Play Drills

Several drills are presented to help your players develop their infield positional skills. We recommend you select the drills that you feel will most effectively benefit your players; then modify the drills to meet the skill level of your players.

(5.1) Infield Teamwork Drill

Age: 9 years and up
Purpose: To teach and refine players' abilities to work together on infield plays

Equipment: One set of bases

Procedure: You will need to instruct and to demonstrate the positional skills and responsibilities to your players. As your players take their infield positions, set up play situations with various outs and baserunning combinations. Hit or throw to different areas of the infield. Your players should field the ball and react by (a) backing-up plays, (b) fielding the ball, and (c) completing the play. This drill should be uncomplicated for younger and less experienced players. Older and more experienced players will be able to think through and execute more complicated plays.

(5.2) Backing-up Drill

Age: 6 years and up

Purpose: To practice backing up other fielders

Equipment: One set of bases

Procedure: Position the fielders in the infield and outfield. You can use a reduced field for this drill by placing the bases 30 ft apart. Call out a fielding situation and throw a ball to begin the action. Have your players move to field the ball, complete the play, and back up other fielders.

(5.3) Individual Position Drill

Age: 9 years and up

Purpose: Provides players with an opportunity to work on skills specific to their defensive positions

Equipment: Gloves, balls

Procedure: Players report to their defensive positions and perform the following skills specific to their position:

Catchers
1. Practice shifting on low pitches in the dirt
2. Practice stance and throws to all bases
3. Practice fielding bunts and pop flies
4. Practice cut-offs and relays
5. Practice tagging runners out

Pitchers
1. Practice covering first base
2. Practice starting double plays
3. Practice bunt coverage
4. Practice cut-offs from the outfield

First Basemen
1. Practice shifting around the bag
2. Practice receiving various types of throws
3. Practice starting double plays
4. Practice bunt coverage
5. Practice cut-offs and relays
6. Practice throwing to pitchers covering first

Second Basemen and Shortstops
1. Practice starting and finishing double plays
2. Practice cut-offs and relays
3. Practice fielding slow rollers
4. Practice fielding all types of ground balls

Third Basemen
1. Practice moving to the right and left
2. Practice slow rollers
3. Practice cut-offs and relays
4. Practice bunt coverage
5. Practice starting double plays

Outfielders
1. Practice judging and fielding fly balls
2. Practice fielding ground balls and throwing to the cut-off players

(5.4) Pop-ups for Catchers Drill

Age: 9 years and up

Purpose: To give catchers practice on pop-ups

Equipment: Catching equipment, bat, softballs

Procedure: Hit or throw pop-ups to catchers in full gear. Give constructive feedback to the catcher's fielding attempts.

(5.5) Tag Plays at Home Drill

Age Group: 9 years and up

Purpose: To teach catchers the proper method of tagging out runners who are attempting to score

Equipment: Catching equipment, home plate

Procedure: The catcher wears full gear and assumes a position by home plate as if receiving a throw. The catcher's left foot should be placed on the front edge of the base so that runners can see the back half of the base. Have runners slide into home plate. Other fielders or a coach should throw the ball, timed barely to beat the runner, to the catcher. The catcher then tries to tag out the runner. Rotate catchers after 10 throws. Initially, have your catchers practice this drill without runners. The runners can be added after catchers become more skilled in executing tags at home plate.

(5.6) Catchers Throwing From the Stance Drill

Age Group: 9 years and up

Purpose: To teach catchers how to throw to bases

Equipment: Home plate, bases, balls, gloves, catcher's gear

Procedure: Set up bases and position players. Catchers should wear gear for this drill even though the ball should be pitched slow. Catchers receive pitches and throw to the bases. Rotate catchers and reposition fielders after 10 throws.

Chapter 6:
Playing the Outfield

Introduction:
The Importance of an Outfield

Outfielders are an important part of a team's overall defense. In fact, they are the last line of defense and cover the largest area of the playing field. Consequently, every ball hit to the outfield is a potential *big play* for the offense; therefore, outfielders must be alert, communicate with each other, be ready to back-up infielders, and relay the ball to the infield quickly. However, beginning softball players often lack the strength to hit to the outfield consistently; as a result, outfielders usually make plays less often than infielders, and this dead time can lead to outfielders not concentrating on the game. Keeping your outfielders actively involved in the game, even if they are not directly involved in a play, is a real challenge to your coaching abilities. Let them know that each time they hustle after the ball, shout encouragement to their teammates, and back up players, they are contributing to the total defense of the team.

The following outfield responsibilities and aspects of defensive play are covered in this chapter:

- Positioning outfielders
- The outfield ready position
- Catching fly balls
- Fielding outfield grounders
- Throwing to the infield
- Communicating in the outfield
- Backing up plays
- Outfield play drills

Positioning Outfielders

Where outfielders are positioned depends upon the type of softball played: Fast-pitch softball allows *three* outfielders; slow-pitch softball allows *four* outfielders. Regardless of the number of outfielders, your players should understand the areas of the outfield: *right field*, *center field*, and *left field*. Explain that right field extends from the first-base foul line over near to second base; center field is the middle part of the outfield; and left field extends from the third-base foul line over near to second base (see Figure 6-1). For slow-pitch softball, a fourth area, called *short field*, is the shallow part of the outfield from behind the shortstop to behind the second baseman (see Figure 6-2).

Fig. 6-1

Fig. 6-2

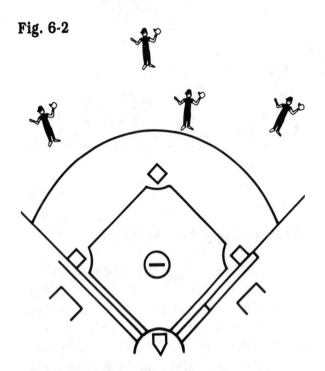

Fig. 6-3

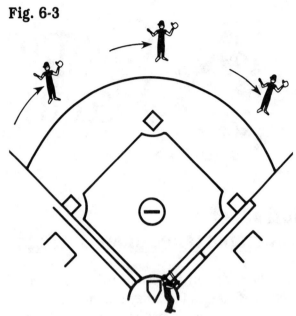

Positioning for Fast-Pitch

In fast-pitch softball, the three outfielders are positioned in left field, center field, and right field and should be able to see the entire infield, including the pitcher, the catcher, and the batter. Tell your players that the better they can see all players on the field, the better they will be able to play their positions.

Explain to your players that there is no predetermined method for playing their positions. The strength of the hitter, the game situation, and the condition of the playing field are some of the factors which will determine exactly where they play, and these factors must be evaluated during each game. However, some general rules can be used to guide the positioning of your outfielders.

Generally, outfielders should play farther back for strong hitters and closer to the infield for weak hitters. Left-handed hitters pose another problem because they tend to hit to the right side of the field. Therefore, when a left-handed hitter comes to bat, shift the outfield over toward right field, as shown in Figure 6-3.

Positioning for Slow-Pitch

Because slow-pitch softball allows four outfielders, there are two different methods of positioning outfielders. In the first method three outfielders are positioned as in fast-pitch and the fourth outfielder, called a *short fielder*, or *rover*, plays the short-field position. Explain that short fielders are responsible for fielding short fly balls hit into the shallow outfield. Generally, short fielders play up the middle or to the left of second base for right-handed hitters, and shift to the right side of second base for left-handed hitters, as shown in Figure 6.4.

Fig. 6-4

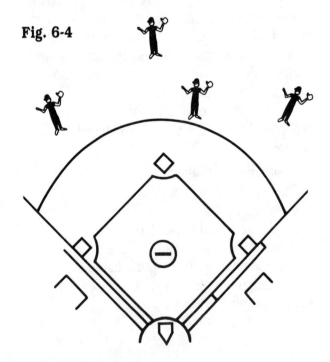

The second method in slow-pitch positions all four outfielders across the outfield, as shown in Figure 6-5. This means the left fielder and right fielder can play closer to the foul lines, and the other outfielders can play to the right and left side of second base. This is a particularly effective method for beginning slow-pitch leagues.

The Outfield Ready Position

When your players understand where to play, they will need to learn how to field balls hit to the outfield. The ready position for outfielders is similar to the ready position for infielders; the difference, shown in Figure 6-6, is that outfielders should not bend down as much as infielders. By standing upright, keeping the knees flexed, arms relaxed, and their weight balanced on the balls of their feet, outfielders will be ready to run and field balls. But, if they bend over too much, they will have to stand up in this ready position before moving to make a play.

Catching Fly Balls

The fundamentals for catching fly balls have been covered in chapters 4 and 5. Only those fac-

Fig. 6-5

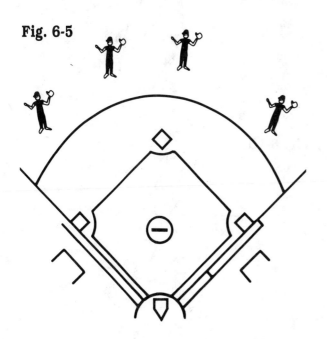

Fig. 6-6

tors which pertain particularly to outfielders are discussed here.

Instruct your outfielders to be alert and always ready to make a play. The sooner they are in position and ready to play, the better they will be able to make any adjustments necessary to catch the ball. Consequently, if they do not hustle, they could be out of position and will not be able to field fly balls. A good drill to practice setting up in the ready position, moving to the ball, and catching fly balls is the Fielding Fly Balls Drill (6.1).

Playing alertly and hustling are also important points to consider, not only for your players, but for you as a coach. Lazy players can cause others to play the same way just as highly motivated players can influence other players to hustle. So set an example: Be enthusiastic and show some hustle yourself. Praise your players and encourage players to praise others who hustle and work hard.

Judging Fly Balls

Judging the flight of fly balls is a difficult skill to teach beginning softball players. Travelling farther than expected and curving across the field, fly balls can be deceiving. There is no easy way to learn how to judge fly balls. Some guides for judging fly balls were presented in chapter 4, but the best way to learn this skill is through practice and experience.

Wind
A strong wind can be particularly annoying for beginning players, so remind them to check the

speed and direction of the wind each inning (see Figure 6-7). If the wind is blowing from home plate to the outfield, the ball will travel farther, so your players should play slightly deeper than usual. If the wind is blowing from the outfield toward home plate, the ball will stall out, so your players should play slightly closer to the infield.

Because the wind can blow the ball around, remind your players that it is easier to catch a ball running forward than running backward. Therefore, whether they play deeper or closer than usual, the ball should not get beyond them. Remember to always follow the principal rule of fielding: *keep the ball in front.*

To emphasize these points, try out the following exercise: Have your players run forward about 50 ft and catch a fly ball at the end of the run. Then have them run backward and catch a fly ball. Your players will soon realize the importance of keeping the ball in front.

Sunlight
Bright sun can also disturb outfielders, making easy plays quite difficult. By holding up the glove to shade the eyes, as shown in Figure 6-8, outfielders can block out the sun and be ready to reach out and catch fly balls. But, be sure your players know not to block out both the sun and the ball; they still need to watch the ball until it is caught.

By now, your players should be able to tell you that using two hands is the best way to catch a

Fig. 6-8

ball (see Figure 6-9) because (a) it helps secure the catch, and (b) it sets up the throw by gripping the ball while it is in the glove. Even so, it is a long way to the outfield fence, and you may need to remind them to use two hands every time they catch a ball.

Fly Balls Falling in Front

No matter how fast a player can run, some balls will still fall in front of them. The best method for catching such low balls while running is to use the *basket catch*, holding out the glove about waist height with the palms facing up (see Figure 6-10). To secure the ball in the glove, show your

Fig. 6-9

Fig. 6-7

Fig. 6-10

players how to bring the glove with both hands in to the body, as shown in Figure 6-11.

Because the basket catch is often used to catch balls on the run, it is a difficult skill for beginning players. Wait until your players are able to run and catch well before teaching the basket catch; then use the Basket Catch Drill (6.2) to practice this skill.

Fielding Outfield Grounders

As mentioned earlier, the outfield is a large area to cover, and each ball not fielded correctly is a big help to the offensive team. Because of this, it is important for outfielders to field ground balls cleanly, to throw to the infield quickly, and to hold runners to as few bases as possible. The best method for blocking, fielding, and throwing ground balls in the outfield is called the *blocking position*. To teach the blocking position, follow Figure 6-12, and show your players how to (a) move to the ball, (b) bend down on the glove-side knee, and (c) place the glove between the legs.

After fielding, the ball can be thrown back to the infield in a continuous motion. Follow the illustration in Figure 6-13 to show your players how to stand up and step into the throw. Use the Outfield Ground Ball-Fly Ball Drill (6.3) to practice fielding and throwing in the outfield.

Throwing to the Infield

Once the ball is fielded, it needs to be thrown with an overhand motion to the infield. Throwing sidearm will cause the ball to curve slightly, making it inaccurate and difficult to catch; but an overhand throw will ensure a straight and more accurate throw (see Figure 6-14).

Also, throw so that the ball gets into the infield quickly. The fastest way to get the ball to the infield is to use a *relay* (explained in chapter 7, Team Defense) with several low, straight throws, rather than one long, high-arching throw. High

Fig. 6-13

Fig. 6-11

BRING GLOVE INTO THE BODY

Fig. 6-14

Fig. 6-12

throws go a long distance but also take a long time, thus allowing a runner to reach another base. Long, high throws also place great stress on the arm and shoulder and, after several throws, could cause the arm to become sore.

Communicating in the Outfield

It is essential to teach teamwork and communication among players at this level. Not only will overall team play improve, but your players will also learn social skills, such as listening and cooperating with others. Also, communicating effectively does not just happen; it is a technique which requires repeated practice using drills such as the Outfield Teamwork Drill (6.4).

Rather than using long, detailed sentences, teach your players to use short statements or one word signals such as, "Mine" or "Relay to shortstop" (see Figure 6-15). Long sentences take too much time and confuse players, whereas short statements provide accurate information quickly, enhancing performance.

Backing Up Plays

Even when your outfielders are not making a play, they can contribute to the overall performance of the team by backing up other fielders, especially the outfielder next to them. Backing-up can also be hazardous if not done correctly, and safety should be a primary concern for you as a coach.

Assignments for Backing Up the Infield

To ensure safety and enhance outfield teamwork, follow the suggested back-up assignments for outfielders listed below (see Figure 6-16):

- Right fielders are responsible for backing up plays at first base and for backing up the second baseman.
- Right center fielders are responsible for backing up plays at second base and the second baseman.

Fig. 6-15

"I have it!"

PLAYERS CAN COMMUNICATE BEFORE . . .

"I thought you would catch it!"

. . . OR AFTER

Fig. 6-16

- Left center fielders are responsible for backing up plays at second base and for backing up the shortstop.
- Left fielders are responsible for backing up plays at third base and the third baseman.
- Shortfielders back up the second baseman or shortstop and back up plays at second base.

Back-Up Positioning

Now that your players know which fielders to back up, they will need to be shown how to position themselves when backing up other fielders. Moving about 20 ft behind the fielder or base to be backed up, as shown in Figure 6-17, will provide enough distance between both players to catch passed balls. If positioned too closely, they will have trouble seeing passed balls and may not have enough time to react.

Outfield Play Drills

(6.1) Fielding Fly Balls Drill

Age: 9 years and up

Purpose: To develop and to refine the skills needed to run after and catch fly balls

Equipment: Balls, gloves

Procedure: Line up the fielders in an open grass field or outfield area. The player at the front of the line moves from the other players to a posi-

Fig. 6-17

tion where he or she can catch fly balls you hit or throw. Have the fielder throw the ball back to you while the next player moves into position. Be sure to hit or throw the balls in different directions with various speeds and arches.

(6.2) Basket Catch Drill

Age: 9 years and up

Purpose: To develop the skills needed to catch a fly ball on the run using a basket catch

Equipment: Balls, gloves

Procedure: Line up the players about 50 ft from the coach. The coach should be at a right angle to the players. Instruct your players to run across the field as you throw easy fly balls straight ahead and to catch these flies using the basket catch. (The right angle enables you to see how well your players are able to perform the basket catch.) We recommend that you begin throwing low, easy fly balls to the players. As your players improve in this skill, you can adjust the height and difficulty of the fly balls. The importance of throwing balls straight ahead is that the players, positioned 50 ft away, will have to run to reach and catch the ball.

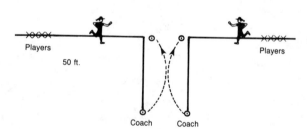

(6.3) Outfield Ground Ball, Fly Ball Drill

Age: 9 years and up

Purpose: To work on outfielding fundamentals

Equipment: Balls, gloves, bats

Procedure: Position your players throughout the outfield and hit various fly balls and ground balls for them to field. Encourage your players to move to the ball quickly rather than waiting for the ball.

(6.4) Outfield Teamwork Drill

Age: 12 and up

Purpose: To teach outfielders to work together

Equipment: Balls, gloves, bat, bases

Procedure: Place one set of outfielders in defensive positions, and place extra outfielders in the infield to receive throws. Tell them that an imaginary runner is on base. The outfielder who will play the ball is not told where the runner is. As the outfielder turns away, the coach signals the location of the runner, the number of outs, and the score. (More than one runner can be on base.) Hit balls to the outfielders from behind second base and have the outfielder nearest the fielder catching the ball call where to throw the ball.

Chapter 7:
Team Defense

Introduction: Working Together

The previous chapters described how to perform, teach, and practice individual softball skills. You will be coaching a softball team, however, so part of your job as a coach will be to teach your players team defensive situations. Softball truly is a team sport and few plays can be accomplished by players working alone. Working together as a team requires cooperation with other players and a willingness to follow the directions you provide. For many players, this may be their first experience playing on a team, and the manner in which you teach teamwork and cooperation will have a lasting effect on their attitude about team sports. We strongly recommend that you teach teamwork using a positive approach, considering the needs of the players on your team, rather than considering the outcome of the game. For if your players perform their skills well and work as a team, the winning or losing will take care of itself.

This chapter will help you teach and practice team defensive skills by presenting the following topics:

• Defensive playing strategies
• Force-outs
• Bunt coverage
• Fly ball coverage
• Steal coverage
• Relays
• Cut-offs
• Double plays
• Team defensive drills

Familiarize yourself with these defensive topics and introduce them to your players in the order presented. Your players will benefit little from double-play practice unless they are able to field and throw to second base and to first base effectively. Consider the skill level and playing experience of your players when introducing them to team defensive plays. Challenge your players with new skills but proceed slowly and deliberately, according to their abilities and experiences.

Defensive Playing Strategies

It will be helpful to your players if you introduce playing strategies by reviewing the objectives of the offensive and of the defensive teams. They should learn that the offensive team tries to hit the ball, to run the bases, and to score runs; in contrast, the defensive team tries to prevent the offensive team from hitting, from running the bases, and from scoring runs by "putting out" that team.

Explain that the defensive team uses certain playing *strategies* to make outs and to control the offensive team. These strategies can become quite complicated and confusing for beginning players.

Rather than teaching beginning players several specific plays for specific situations, we recommend you teach a few general rules which govern defensive playing strategy. Once your athletes understand the general rules of defensive playing strategy, they will be able to apply these rules to specific situations.

Fig. 7-1

"Strategies? Where should I throw the ball?"

Fig. 7-2

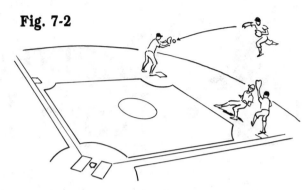

RULE 1: HOLD RUNNERS AT A BASE

Fig. 7-3

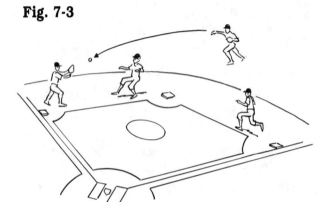

RULE 2: THROW AHEAD OF RUNNER

Introducing your players to softball game strategy need not be time-consuming nor a distraction from practicing fundamental skills. In fact, practice is the best time to learn strategy. By using the Playing Strategy Drill (7.1) during practices, you can teach your players softball skills and softball strategy.

Rule 1: Hold the Runner

The first rule of softball strategy is to keep each base runner from advancing to the next base (see Figure 7-2). This rule is in effect each time a pitch is thrown or a play is made. Of course, the best way to hold a runner is to put out the batter before he or she reaches first base. Stress to your players that holding the runner to a base is the most important rule to follow.

Rule 2: Throw Ahead of the Runner

Demonstrate to your team how throwing ahead of the runner helps to put out the runner or prevent the runner from advancing, as shown in Figure 7-3. Stress to your team that Rule 2 and

Rule 1 work together in helping them control the offensive team.

Rule 3: Throw to a Central Position

Sometimes your players will not be able to throw ahead of a runner but can still throw to a central position such as second base or the pitcher in order to prevent runners from advancing. For example, if a ball is hit to the outfield, and a runner on second base runs to third base, the best play would be to throw the ball to the third baseman, second baseman, or to the pitcher (see Figure 7-4).

Rule 4: Make the Sure Out

The fourth rule of softball playing strategy is to get the sure out. It is better to make a sure out than to try for an out your players are not certain they can make, even if a runner moves to another base or scores a run. For example, when runners are at first base and third base, and a ball is hit to the shortstop, as presented in Figure 7-5,

Fig. 7-4

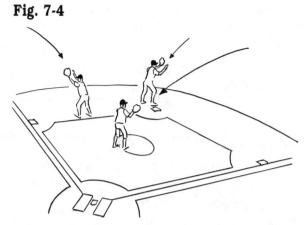

RULE 3: THROW TO A CENTRAL POSITION

Fig. 7-5

RULE 4: MAKE THE SURE OUT

the run at home plate would be difficult to make, so the out should be made at second base.

Rule 5: Make More Than One Out

The final rule of softball defensive strategy is to try to make more than one out each play (see Figure 7-6). Tell your players that making more than one out is the least important of all the defensive strategy rules and should be followed only after a sure out is made.

This is especially true when players bobble or mishandle a ball. When this occurs, they should make the first *sure* out before attempting to make a more difficult out as part of a double play.

Your players will understand Rule 5 better as you explain *double plays*. Double plays can be made when (a) a fly ball is caught for an out and is thrown back to a base to force out a runner; or (b) the second baseman or shortstop fields a ball and touches second base to force out a runner, then throws to first base to force out the batter. The most common double plays involve the

Fig. 7-6

RULE 5: MAKE MORE THAN ONE OUT

second baseman and shortstop working together and are explained thoroughly later in this chapter.

Teaching Progression for Softball Strategies

1. Teach Rule 1. This will help your players understand the objectives of defensive play.
2. Teach Rules 2 and 3. These rules will help your players understand where to throw the ball to best accomplish their defensive objectives.
3. Teach Rule 4. Rule 4 establishes the priority for making outs. Always encourage your players to make the sure out.
4. Teach Rule 5. This is the least important of all defensive strategies for beginning softball players. Teach this rule after your players have demonstrated the ability to make multiple plays.
5. Practice making plays based upon these rules in game situations.

Force-Outs

Force-outs, if explained correctly, should not be difficult for beginning players to understand. Simply explain that a force-out occurs when a defensive player catches a ball and touches a base before the runner. (See chapter 11 in the Planning Guide for a more complete description of force-outs.)

To become proficient at making force-outs, your players must learn the positional assignments described in chapter 5, and they must learn how to receive throws from other players by practicing the Force-out Practice Drill (7.2). As a general guideline, force-outs are made by the fielder responsible for that base. You can help your players understand their force-out assignments by demonstrating the following situations:

Situation	Player Responsible
1. Force-out at first base	First baseman
2. Force-out at second base	Second baseman
3. Force-out at third base	Third baseman
4. Force-out at home plate	Catcher

Sometimes a ball is hit so that the fielder responsible for the force-out fields the ball. When this happens, two plays are possible. First, the fielder responsible for the force-out fields the ball and also makes the out (see Figure 7-7). Explain that this should be done only if the ball is hit close to the base.

Second, the player closest to the base fields the ball and throws to the player responsible for backing up that base. These coverage responsibilities are as follows:

Situation	Player Responsible
1. Force-out at first base when the first baseman fields the ball	Pitcher or second baseman
2. Force-out at second base when the second baseman fields the ball	Shortstop
3. Force-out at third base when the third baseman fields the ball	Pitcher or shortstop
4. Force-out at home plate when the catcher fields the ball	Pitcher

Coaching Points for Force-Outs

1. Have the players cover the bases.
2. Be sure your players are ready to back up other bases.
3. First priority is to catch the ball, then touch the base.

Teaching Progression for Force-Outs

1. Teach how to move to the base and receive the throw.
2. Teach how to back up a base and receive the throw.
3. Begin with easy throws and with players walking through their assignments on shortened base paths.
4. Gradually progress to using balls thrown at regular speeds; then have players run through their assignments on a regulation field.
5. Practice making force-outs in game situations.

Bunt Coverage

Fielding softly hit balls, called *bunts*, is one of the most difficult plays in softball. Because bunts do not roll far, the base runner has more time to reach the base, and the infielders must run in to the ball, leaving bases uncovered. Throws to the bases are often hurried and inaccurate, so outfielders must run in to back up the infield.

Assigning specific responsibilities to each infielder will help your players know exactly how to play bunts and will help to eliminate confusion among players. Consequently, practicing bunt coverage using a drill such as the Bunt Reaction Drill 7.3 is essential for developing a solid defense.

Fig. 7-7

Player Positions

The positioning of your players will depend upon their fielding area and where the ball is bunted. As shown in Figure 7-8, bunts are usually placed between home plate and the pitching circle, and along the foul lines. Therefore, your players will need to move toward these areas when a bunt is anticipated.

The difficulty of fielding bunts is increased when they are hit along the foul lines. Players must then decide whether the ball will remain in *fair territory* or will roll into *foul territory*. If it is clear that a ball will roll foul, teach your players not to touch it until after it rolls foul. This will place a strike on the batter, reducing the probability of other bunt attempts. Beware, however, bunts that roll close to the foul line can be deceiving. As a general rule, if the ball is close to the foul line but not rolling foul, field the ball and try for the sure out.

When you notice a bunt situation, move the third baseman and first baseman into the shallow infield where they can charge bunts (see Figure 7-9). By staying close to the foul line, they can judge whether the ball will stay fair or roll foul.

Pitchers and catchers also have fielding responsibilities in bunt situations (see Figure 7-10). Pitchers cover the area directly in front of the pitching circle, and catchers cover the area immediately in front of home plate.

Because the first baseman and third baseman move in, the shortstop and second baseman

Fig. 7-9

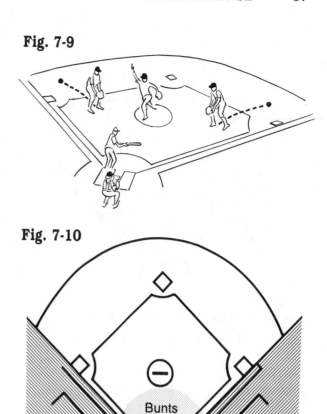

Fig. 7-10

must cover all three bases. When there is no runner on second base, have the shortstop move over to second base, and the second baseman move over to first base as shown in Figure 7-11.

When a runner is on second base, the object of the defense is to prevent the runner from moving to third base. In this situation, the shortstop

Fig. 7-8

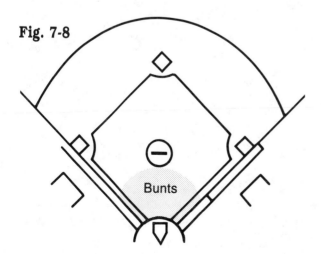

Fig. 7-11

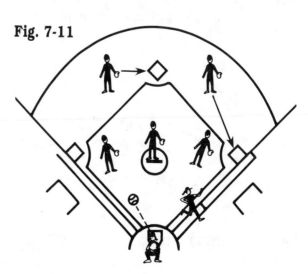

Fig. 7-12

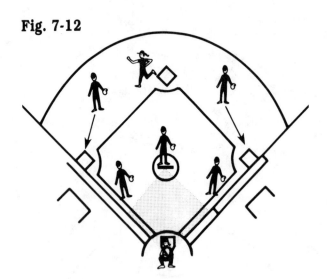

covers third base rather than second base, as illustrated in Figure 7-12.

Fielding the Bunt

More than one player may be able to field a bunt, so to avoid confusion, a priority system should be used. This priority system depends upon where the ball is bunted and who reaches the ball first. When a bunt is hit to a player's coverage area, that player has priority for fielding the bunt. However, the best priority system is to teach the player who reaches the ball first to call out "Mine," (see Figure 7-13), and for the other fielders to leave the ball alone.

Coaching Points for Fielding Bunts

1. Demonstrate the responsibilities and coverage areas for each position.
2. Demonstrate the back-up responsibilities of the second baseman and shortstop.

Fig. 7-13

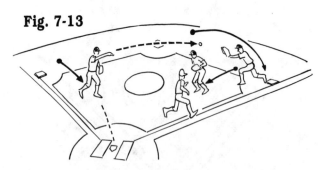

CALL FOR BUNT, FIELD, AND THROW FOR THE OUT

3. Encourage your players to field the ball properly and to throw accurately.

Teaching Progression for Fielding Bunts

1. Teach your players their responsibilities, coverage areas, and back-up responsibilities.
2. Walk the players through fielding bunts and throwing to bases.
3. Gradually progress to fielding bunts and throwing to bases at regular speeds.
4. Practice fielding bunts in game situations.

Fly Ball Coverage

Fly balls travel across several positions, so more than one player may be able to field a fly. In other situations, fly balls hit to one area may be played easier by another fielder. To eliminate any confusion concerning which players field fly balls, your team will need to use a priority system similar to the one used for fielding bunts. This system is shown in Figures 7-14 to 7-19 and explained below:

1. When fly balls are hit to left-center field or right-center field, center fielders have priority over other outfielders.
2. Because it is easier to catch a ball while running forward than running backward, outfielders have priority over infielders.

Fig. 7-14

CENTER FIELDERS HAVE PRIORITY OVER OTHER OUTFIELDERS

Fig. 7-15

OUTFIELDERS HAVE PRIORITY OVER INFIELDERS

Fig. 7-17

FOR HITS BEHIND FIRST OR THIRD BASE SHORTSTOPS OR SECOND BASEMEN HAVE PRIORITY

3. Because pitchers and catchers are usually not in a good position to field infield fly balls, the other infielders have priority over pitchers and catchers.
4. The second baseman and shortstop will have a better angle to see and to field fly balls hit behind first base and third base than will the first baseman and third baseman. When fly balls are hit behind first or third base, the second baseman and shortstop have priority.
5. Catchers have priority for pop-ups which are near or behind home plate.
6. Because the pitcher's follow-through makes it difficult to move and to field fly balls, pitchers should call for pop-ups only when necessary.

Fig. 7-18

CATCHERS HAVE PRIORITY FOR BALLS HIT NEAR HOME PLATE

Fig. 7-16

OTHER INFIELDERS HAVE PRIORITY OVER PITCHERS AND CATCHERS

Fig. 7-19

PITCHING FOLLOW-THROUGH MAKES IT DIFFICULT TO REACT QUICKLY

Coaching Points for Fly Ball Coverage

1. Teach players to watch the ball.
2. Teach players to call for the ball.
3. Teach players to know their fielding areas and responsibilities.

Teaching Progression for Fly Ball Coverage

1. Teach positional coverage areas.
2. Practice catching easy fly balls thrown from short distances.
3. Progress to calling for and catching more difficult fly balls on a regulation outfield.
4. Practice fly ball coverage in game situations.

Steal Coverage

Most players will be familiar with the term *steal*, but they may not know that runners stealing a base must be tagged out rather than forced out. Also, stealing is allowed only in fast-pitch softball after the pitcher has released the ball, but never in slow-pitch softball. This makes stealing quite risky for the base runner.

However, some players will try to steal bases, so both the catcher and the fielder must act quickly. Teach your fielders to do two things when they see a base runner attempting to steal a base: (a) move to the base, and (b) call out "Steal!" (see Figure 7-20).

The Throw

The distance between home plate and second base makes throwing to second base particular-

Fig. 7-20

Steal!

ly difficult for beginning catchers; but it is the base most often stolen. Always play it safe! Teach catchers not to throw unless they are sure they can throw the runner out. The best way to throw from the crouched position is to step into the throw just as outfielders throw from the blocking position. Stress for low, accurate throws. You cannot risk having the ball get by the fielder, allowing the runner to advance to another base.

Backing-Up

There is always the possibility that throws will get by the fielder, so every fielder has back-up responsibilities. The shortstop backs up second base; the third baseman covers third base; the first baseman backs up home plate; outfielders move in; and the pitcher should be ready to back up the next possible play.

Coaching Points for Steal Coverage

1. Position players slightly behind and to the side of the base.
2. Emphasize watching the ball, making the catch, and tagging the runner.
4. Other players should move into the back-up positions.

Teaching Progression for Steal Coverage

1. Teach the coverage areas and back-up positions.
2. Demonstrate how to bend down, place the glove in the path of the runner, and move away after the tag is made.
3. Practice covering steal attempts by walking through steal situations on shortened base paths.
4. Gradually progress to practicing steal coverage at regular speed on regulation base paths.
5. Practice steal coverage in game situations.

Relays

When a ball is hit to the outfield, the best method for throwing it back to the infield is to use a *relay*

Fig. 7-21

in which several players work together. Relaying the ball is quite simple for beginning players to learn. Have them move into the shallow outfield, receive the throw, and throw the ball to the infield (see Figure 7-21).

Relaying to Home Plate

More than one relay player may be needed when balls are hit deep to the outfield and thrown to home plate. In these situations, players who are free of responsibilities move into position and become additional relay players.

Coaching Points for Relay Throws

1. Be sure all fielders move into relay and back-up positions.
2. Emphasize accurate throws and sure catches.
3. Encourage relay players to throw using the hop step.

Teaching Progression for Relay Throws

1. Begin practicing relay throws from moderate distances with easy throws.
2. Gradually increase the distance and speed of the relay throws.
3. Practice relay throws in competitive situations.

Cut-Offs

Sometimes a throw will need to be caught or *cut off* before it reaches its target. For example, if it is obvious a runner will score before a throw reaches the catcher, the ball should be cut off in front of home plate (see Figure 7-22). Cutting off a throw could also help throw out runners who are trying to take extra bases. Two drills which are especially useful for practicing cut-offs are the Cut-off and Relay Drill (7.4) and the Team Throwing for Points Drill (7.5).

Position cut-off players about 10 ft ahead of the base where the play is to be made. Most often, throws will be cut off at third base and home plate. For throws to third base, the shortstop should be the cut-off, and for throws to home plate the pitcher should be the cut-off.

The third baseman and the catcher can help the cut-off players by calling out, "Come through" when the ball should not be cut off or "Cut off," when the ball should be cut off (see Figure 7-23). Other players may become excited and want to help by calling out, but you should discourage this. The third baseman and catcher are the only players who know if the play can be made and are the only players who should make the call.

Coaching Points for Cut-Offs

1. Emphasize accurate throws and catches.
2. Emphasize moving into position before the ball arrives.

Fig. 7-22

Fig. 7-23

Fig. 7-24

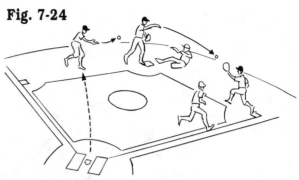

3. Teach your fielders to practice calling, "Come through" and "Cut-off."
4. Emphasize making the tag-out properly when the ball does come through.

Teaching Progression for Cut-Offs

1. Explain the purpose of cut-offs to your players.
2. Demonstrate the proper cut-off positions.
3. Demonstrate the proper cut-off calls, "Come through" and "Cut-off."
4. Practice cut-offs from short distances with easy throws.
5. Gradually progress to practicing cut-offs from regulation distances with throws at regular speed.
6. Practice cut-offs in game situations.

Double Plays

Remind your players that *double play* is the term used for making two outs in one play. The most common double play is when the shortstop and the second baseman work together to complete a force-out at second base and then throw to first base to force-out the batter. Of course, this can only happen if (a) a runner is on first base, and (b) a hit forces the runner to second base, as illustrated in Figure 7-24. Several useful drills for teaching and practicing double plays are the Receiving Tosses Drill (7.6), the Ground Balls into Double Play Drill (7.7), the Double Play Practice Drill (7.8), and the Double Play Practice with Runners Drill (7.9).

Covering Second Base

Explain that the second baseman and shortstop work together to cover second base. The second baseman covers the base when the ball is fielded by the shortstop or the third baseman. The shortstop covers the base when the ball is fielded by the second baseman or first baseman. If the pitcher fields the ball, the player with the best position should move to second base.

Making the Double Play

Learning how to make double plays will be enjoyable if you teach each component in its proper sequence, as illustrated in Figures 7-25 to 7-27. First, teach your players to toss the ball so it is caught before the fielder reaches the base. Second, after catching the ball, teach your players to touch and step away from the base. The final part of this sequence is to throw to first base accurately.

Coaching Points for Double Plays

1. Shortstops cover second base if the ball is fielded on the first-base side of the field; second basemen cover second base if the ball is fielded on the third-base side of the field.

Fig. 7-25

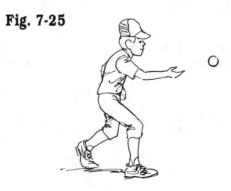

Fig. 7-26

Fig. 7-27

2. Toss the ball underhand, and so the fielder catches it before reaching the base.
3. Touch second base for the first out, step away from the base, and throw to first for the second out.

Teaching Progression for Double Plays

1. Begin by having infielders practice throwing from second base to first base.
2. Practice tossing to the player covering second base.
3. Practice receiving the toss, touching and stepping away from second base, and throwing to first base.
4. Practice with bases close together, and then practice from the regulation distance.
5. Practice double plays in game situations.

Team Defense Drills

In addition to the drills referenced in this chapter, the Three-Player Drill (7.10), the Reduced Playing Field Drill (7.11), the Game Situation Drill (7.12), the Infield and Outfield Drill (7.13), and the Practice Game Drill (7.14) will help your players practice working together as a defensive unit. Feel free to modify these drills when necessary to better aid your coaching and the skill development of your softball players. The Planning Guide section of this book provides realistic application of these drills for skill development and for team practice leading up to the first game.

(7.1) Playing Strategy Drill

Age: 9 years and up

Purpose: To introduce and to explain playing strategies to your players

Equipment: None

Procedures: To maximize your practice time, divide your players among your coaches. Place your players at each position on the field and present Playing Strategy Rules 1 through 5 (pp. 63-65) by setting up specific playing situations. Explain how these rules would specify where the ball should be thrown and why these rules apply. Introduce the rules in a progressive manner, and practice several situations for each rule before moving to the next rule.

(7.2) Force-out Practice Drill

Age: 9 years and up

Purpose: To teach and practice making force-outs at each base

Equipment: Gloves, balls, bases

Procedure: Introduce and explain force-outs to your players. Divide your players among your coaches to maximize your practice time. Set up situations where force-outs would occur at first base, second base, third base, and home plate. Throw or hit ground balls and fly balls to your players and have them throw for the force-out. It is important that you help your beginning players learn where to throw for force-outs by presenting them with specific situations and by explaining where to throw for the force-out.

(7.3) Bunt Reaction Drill

Age: 9 years and up

Purpose: To develop skills required for playing the bunt

Equipment: Balls, bats, gloves

Procedure: Divide your team in half: Have one half work with one coach while the other half works with another coach. If there is only one coach, have your players double up on positions and take turns fielding. Place your fielders in their infield positions (including pitcher and catcher). The pitcher will pitch to the batter (coach), who squares to bunt. The coach may also simulate bunt situations by indicating the number of outs, number of runners on base, and the bases which the runners occupy. When the ball is bunted, instruct your players to charge and field the ball, to move to the proper bases, and to back up other positions. Be sure to bunt the ball in all directions of the infield. Have players switch positions after the ball has been bunted three times in each direction (third-base line, first-base line, and straight ahead).

(7.4) Cut-off and Relay Drill

Age: 9 years and up

Purpose: To develop relay-throwing skills

Equipment: Balls, gloves

Procedure: Players work in groups of five. Arrange your players in a straight line with each player 60 to 70 ft apart. Beginning players should be positioned closer than more experienced players. Have the first player throw to the second player, who throws to the third player. Once the last player in line catches the ball, the process starts again in the opposite direction.

(7.5) Team Throwing for Points Drill

Age: 12 years and up

Purpose: To develop throwing accuracy

Equipment: Gloves, softballs, infield set-up

Procedure: Assign a player to each position on the field. Teach your players the number of their position (as indicated in the numbering system of an official scorebook: pitcher-1, catcher-2, first baseman-3, second baseman-4, third baseman-5, shortstop-6, left fielder-7, center fielder-8, right fielder-9). Have the pitcher begin the drill by executing a skip and throw to the player whose number you call out. Because beginning players may have difficulty remembering the number of their fielding position, call out the name of the player or the position that fielder is playing.

(7.6) Receiving Tosses Drill

Age Group: 9 years and up

Purpose: To practice receiving tosses near second base and making tosses from different areas using shortstop and second base positions

Equipment: Ball, base, gloves

Procedure: The shortstop gets in position near second base and receives tosses from the second baseman, who practices making throws from different areas of that position. Following 10 to 15 tosses, the second baseman stays near second base and receives throws from the shortstop.

(7.7) Ground Ball into Double Play Drill

Age: 12 years and up

Purpose: Provides practice for performing double plays

Equipment: First and second base, gloves, ball

*Procedure:*Have one player stand near the pitcher's mound and throw a variety of ground balls and short hops to the shortstop and second baseman. Let both infielders practice fielding, tossing the ball to start the double play, and executing the necessary pivot and throw to first base.

(7.8) Double Play Practice Drill

Age: 9 years and up

Purpose: To introduce, to teach, and to practice double plays

Equipment: Three bases, gloves, balls, bat

Procedure: Place first and second base half their usual distance apart. The shortstop, second baseman, and first baseman stand in their usual positions in relation to the bases. Toss ground balls to the shortstop, who fields and throws to the second baseman, who throws to first base to complete the double play.

(7.9) Double Play Practice with Runner Drill

Age: 12 years and up

Purpose: To practice double plays in a game-like situation and to give players practice running

Equipment: Infield set-up, balls, bat, gloves, helmets

Procedure: Third basemen, shortstops, second basemen, first basemen, catchers, and pitchers are positioned in the infield. All other players are runners and should wear helmets. One runner starts at first base and one runner starts in the batter's box. As you hit ground balls to the infielders, the runner at home plate runs to first, and the runner on first base runs to second base. Instruct the runners to run off to the side of the bases to avoid running into the fielders or into the throw. After each play, the runner at first base remains at first base and prepares to run to second base. The other runner moves from the bases and waits his or her turn to run from home plate again.

(7.10) Three-Player Drill

Age: 9 years and up

Purpose: To practice all the fundamentals of fielding, throwing, and catching

Equipment: Balls (one for every three players), gloves

Procedure: Arrange the players in a triangle, with players 30 to 40 ft apart. One player rolls various types of ground balls and fly balls to the other two players. Ground balls should vary from fast ground balls and short hops to slow rollers (depending on the age group and skill level).

(7.11) Reduced Playing Field Drill

Age: 9 years and up

Purpose: To explain specifics of softball in a modified setting

Equipment: Three bases, home plate, balls, gloves

Procedure: Set up an infield with bases only 30 ft apart. Have some players take their positions on the field, while other players remain at home plate to be runners. Throw or hit balls to the infielders, who field and throw to complete plays. Rotate players after five throws to each position.

(7.12) Game Situation Drill

Age: 9 years and up

Purpose: Provides players with an opportunity to work on skills specific to their defensive positions

Equipment: None necessary, but can use gloves

Procedure: Position your players at their defensive positions and set up game situations by putting runners on base and calling the number of outs. After each simulation, have your players get into the ready position, imagine another type of game situation, and execute the play. This can be a fun drill for your players, especially if you let your players set up their own game situations.

(7.13) Infield and Outfield Drill

Age: 9 years and up

Purpose: Effective pregame defense practice, or pregame warm-up

Equipment: Complete field, balls, gloves, bat, catcher's equipment

Procedure: Have your players assume their defensive positions. You can design any situation you wish your team to practice. The following is an example of how you could use this drill:

Outfield Phase

- Hit two fly balls and two ground balls to each outfielder. Instruct the outfielders to throw to the infielders as though they were in a real game. Hit several balls to each position.

Infield Phase

- Hit several balls to each infielder. The infielders should throw to first base, second base, or third base. Coaches can call out where to throw the ball.

Double Play Phase

- The procedure continues as described above, but now the infielders practice double plays.

Throw Home Phase

- Hit a final ground ball to each infielder. Instruct the infielder to field the ball and to throw to the catcher at home plate. After catching the ball, the catcher rolls the ball back to the infielder, who charges the ball and throws to first base, then runs off the field.

Completion Phase

• The coach concludes the drill by hitting a pop-up and bunt to the catcher.

7.14 Practice Game Drill

Age: All

Purpose: To practice softball skills in a game setting

Equipment: Balls, complete infield set up, bats, helmets

Procedure: Divide the team in half by selecting two teams of equal ability. Play a game following the rules of your league or organization. Allow each player the opportunity to practice playing two positions. Do not end an inning with 3 outs. Rather, end each inning after each offensive player has batted, even if there are less or more than 3 outs.

Chapter 8: Pitching

Introduction: Pitching Considerations

The names *fast-pitch* softball and *slow-pitch* softball describe the major difference between the two games. In each game, the ball is pitched with an underhand motion; the speed and arc of the ball, however, determine the game style. In fast-pitch softball, the ball is pitched as fast as possible and travels to the catcher virtually in a straight line. In slow-pitch softball, the ball is pitched with high arc to make hitting difficult. Pitching fast is a more precise and complex skill than pitching slow; therefore, the majority of this chapter is devoted to helping coaches develop fast-pitch pitchers.

This chapter covers the following:

- The youth league softball pitcher
- The slow-pitch style
- The fast-pitch style
- Illegal pitches
- Pitching drills

The Youth League Softball Pitcher

Let every player interested in pitching have an opportunity to learn pitching skills. Not every player will be interested, and not all pitchers will be able to pitch in all games; however, every player should be given the opportunity to learn pitching skills. Remember that maturational rates vary among children of similar age. Children who are large, fast, and strong for their age may be later surpassed by children who are shorter, slower, and not as strong at an earlier age. Allowing every player to learn pitching skills will be like planting seeds: Some will grow well this season, and others will grow better in the future. The important point is that each player has the opportunity to learn and to develop this skill.

Consequently, do not channel your players into certain positions based upon how strong, fast, and large they are at a certain age. Encouraging beginning players to experience and to learn skills for all playing positions will not only add to their immediate enjoyment, but will also allow them to adjust and to play positions more suited to their abilities later in life. Two drills which will be helpful in teaching and practicing softball pitching are the Tarp Target Drill (8.1) and the Hit the Mitt Drill (8.2).

The Slow-Pitch Style

Pitching in slow-pitch softball is less complicated than in fast-pitch softball. A good slow-pitch pitcher does not need to strike out batters. In slow-pitch, the object is to make hitting the ball difficult by pitching the ball with an arc at least 6 ft and not more than 12 ft from the ground.

Explain that a slow-pitch with a high arc takes longer to travel farther than a fast-pitch with a short arc. Consequently, during the flight of a slow-pitch ball, even small errors have the time and distance to become exaggerated. Therefore, instruct slow-pitch pitchers to swing the ball along a straight path, releasing it from the fingers with an easy, fluid arm motion (see Figure 8-1).

Fig. 8-1

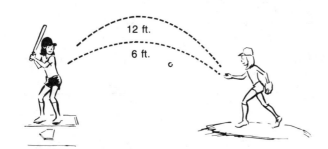

The Fast-Pitch Style

Types of Deliveries

Use the illustrations in Figures 8-2 and 8-3 to demonstrate these pitching styles. The *slingshot* should be a slow backward armswing with a fast forward swing and release. The *windmill* moves the arm completely around the shoulder.

The slingshot is easier to learn and is more accurate for beginning pitchers than the windmill delivery. It is also useful for helping beginning pitchers learn to release the ball properly. Use the slingshot delivery for teaching proper pitching mechanics and release of the pitch. After your players have learned the slingshot delivery well, they will be ready to try the windmill delivery.

Strike Zone

The strike zone in fast-pitch softball is similar to the strike zone in baseball. Explain that the fast-pitch strike zone covers the area of the plate be-

Fig. 8-2

SLINGSHOT PITCH

Fig. 8-3

WINDMILL PITCH

tween the top of the batter's knees to the batter's armpits; the slow-pitch strike zone extends from the top of the shoulders to the knees.

Analysis of an Effective Pitching Delivery

All pitchers use slightly different deliveries because of their different builds and styles. By teaching your players correct and efficient pitching skills rather than making them duplicate a standard pitching style, they will be able to combine these skills to create their own effective pitching style.

Whether a pitcher uses a slingshot or windmill delivery, there are several *checkpoints* you can use to make sure your pitchers develop correct skills for both deliveries. The following five checkpoints are intended as coaching guidelines and should be taught as components of a continuous flowing motion rather than as isolated components of the pitch.

1. The presentation and stance
2. The backswing
3. The downswing
4. The release
5. The follow-through

The Presentation and Stance
The presentation and stance are similar for both the slingshot and windmill deliveries. According to softball rules, the ball must be held stationary in front of the body for at least 1 second, and the

pitcher must have one foot on the pitching rubber (see Figure 8-4).

The pitcher should take advantage of the pitching rubber to get a powerful push-off. The best stance for this is shown in Figure 8-5; the pitcher stands with the push-off foot in front of and touching the rubber and the striding foot in back of or on top of the rubber.

The Backswing
For the slingshot delivery, the arm prepares for the pitch by swinging directly in back of the body, as shown in Figure 8-6. The pitching arm is slightly bent, with the wrist cocked. As the arm swings, the body rocks back on the legs. This rocking motion shifts the body weight backward and forward for a smooth, powerful pitch. If the pitcher's arm is not swung directly back, but off to the side, the ball will be pitched to the side.

Fig. 8-4

Fig. 8-5

Fig. 8-6

Let each pitcher know when his or her arm swing is correct or incorrect and guide the swing until he or she gets the "feel" of a correct backswing.

For the windmill delivery the arm is swung forward and upward with the arm slightly bent and the wrist cocked (see Figure 8-7). In the windmill, rather than rocking back, the front leg is lifted up to stride forward, and the pitcher's weight shifts to the push-off leg.

The Downswing
During the downswing in the slingshot delivery, the body pushes forward, the front leg strides toward home plate, and the arm swings in a downward arc toward the target (see Figure 8-8). The most difficult part of the downswing is stepping directly forward and swinging the ball straight. Again, be sure to guide this phase until your pitchers develop a feel for the downswing.

During the downswing in the windmill delivery, the glove-side foot strides directly toward the

Fig. 8-7

Fig. 8-8

target, the body pushes forward, and the arm swings back and down to complete a circle (see Figure 8-9). As with the slingshot delivery, be sure to check the direction of the front foot and arm.

The Release

Releasing the pitch is similar for both the windmill and slingshot deliveries. Follow Figure 8-10 and demonstrate how to snap the wrist forward and release the ball from the fingers as the back foot leaves the pitching rubber.

The exact point of release will depend upon the pitcher. Each pitcher will develop his or her own release point or several release points for various pitches. You can help your pitchers develop their release by providing the following feedback information:

- If the pitch was low, the ball was probably released too soon.

Fig. 8-9

Fig. 8-10

SLINGSHOT   WINDMILL
RELEASE   RELEASE

- If the pitch was high, the ball was probably released too late.
- If the pitch was to either side of the plate, check the backswing and downswing positions to be sure the ball is swung straight back and forward.

The Follow-through

The follow-through is also similar for the slingshot and windmill deliveries. Remind your pitchers that a good follow-through results from a correct pitch. As shown in Figure 8-11, the pitching arm continues upward comfortably as the push-off leg steps through in front of the striding leg.

Coaching Points for the Slingshot Delivery

1. Develop the proper stance and presentation of the ball.
2. Grip the ball in the normal throwing manner.
3. Swing the ball backward and forward in a straight line.
4. Step toward the target and push off the pitching rubber.
5. Release the ball by snapping the wrist.
6. Follow-through.

Coaching Points for the Windmill Delivery

1. Develop the proper stance and presentation of the ball.

Fig. 8-11

2. Grip the ball in the normal throwing manner.
3. Swing the ball up and around the shoulder.
4. Swing the ball forward and toward the target in a straight line.
5. Step toward the target and push off the pitching rubber.
6. Release the ball by snapping the wrist.
7. Follow-through.

Coaching Progression for the Slingshot Delivery

1. Demonstrate and practice the ready position and presenting the ball.
2. Demonstrate and practice the backswing.
3. Demonstrate and practice the downswing.
4. Combine and practice the backswing and downswing.
5. Demonstrate and practice pushing off the rubber and releasing the ball.
6. Combine and practice all parts of the pitching delivery.
7. Practice pitching easily to a target which is a moderate distance away.
8. Gradually progress to pitching to a catcher from the regulation distance.
9. Practice pitching to batters in game situations.

Teaching Progression for the Windmill Delivery

1. Demonstrate and practice the ready position and presenting the ball.
2. Demonstrate and practice the backswing.

3. Demonstrate and practice the downswing.
4. Combine and practice the backswing and downswing.
5. Demonstrate and practice pushing off the rubber and releasing the ball.
6. Combine and practice all parts of the pitching delivery.
7. Practice pitching easily to a target which is a moderate distance away.
8. Gradually progress to pitching to a catcher from the regulation distance.
9. Practice pitching to batters in game situations.

Illegal Pitches

Explain to your players that according to the rules, the pitch begins when the pitcher makes any wind-up motion after the ball is presented. This means the pitcher must pitch directly to the batter or step off the back of the rubber. Any attempt to distract the batter or prevent the batter from hitting the pitch is illegal, and the umpire will call a ball. Also, if the pitcher, while on the pitching rubber or after stepping in front of the rubber, throws to a base, the umpire will rule the pitch illegal, call a ball, and will allow any base runners to advance one base.

Pitching Drills

The following drills have been designed to develop the skills needed to pitch accurately and consistently. We urge you to modify these skills to the age and skill levels you are coaching in order to develop pitching skills more effectively.

(8.1) Tarp Target Drill
Age Group: 9 years and up
Purpose: To help pitchers develop pitching control and accuracy
Equipment: Tarp, net, or backstop with strike zone target area marked
Procedure: Have pitchers practice delivering

pitches to various spots on the tarp. Pitch from a close distance, then from the regulation pitching distance after they have developed a good pitching motion and ball release.

(8.2) Hit the Mitt Drill

Age Group: 9 years and up

Purpose: To develop a pitcher's ability to throw at specific targets

Equipment: Catching gear, balls

Procedure: Pitchers and catchers get into position at a regulation distance from one another with catchers behind home plate. Have catchers give the pitcher a target by positioning the catching mitt at various positions around home plate. Add batters to this drill after your pitchers have developed adequate accuracy and control.

Chapter 9:
Catching Pitches

Introduction:
A Challenging Position

Catching fast-pitch or slow-pitch softball can be a difficult but challenging position for beginning players. Catchers assume much responsibility for catching pitches and, because they can see the entire field, are counted on to be a team leader. But the catcher must also squat behind the plate for long periods of time, close to the umpire, the batter, and foul balls. Consequently, you may have a high turnover at the catcher position.

The fielding responsibilities of catchers were covered in chapter 5, "Positional Infield Skills." Presented in this chapter are the duties of the catcher as a member of the *battery*, or the duo of the pitcher and catcher; included are the following topics:

- Working with the pitcher
- Catching fast pitches
- Catching slow-pitch softball
- Catching drills

Working With the Pitcher

Explain to your players that the most vital responsibility of catchers is helping the pitcher in any way possible. This includes (a) warming up the pitcher before games, (b) helping detect problems in the pitcher's delivery, and (c) helping pitchers maintain their confidence. Exactly how catchers work with pitchers will depend upon the style of softball played. For example, fast-pitch softball allows stealing and bunting, so the job of the fast-pitch catcher is more demanding than for the slow-pitch catcher.

Catching Fast Pitches

The Catcher's Stance

The first stance, shown in Figure 9-1, is a squatting position with the feet about hip-width apart and the glove-side (back) foot slightly behind the throwing side (front) foot. To get into this position, have your players stand with the feet spread apart, the toe of the back foot even with the heel of the front foot; then, have them simply squat down. With the feet spread apart and in the front-to-back position, it is easy to remain balanced, to shift to block pitches, and to step and throw. However, this position places great stress on the upper legs, causing catchers to become sore and tired.

The second stance is a kneeling position which eliminates much of the stress from the upper legs

Fig. 9-1

CATCHER'S SQUATTING STANCE

but does not provide as much mobility for the catcher. As illustrated in Figure 9-2, the glove-side knee rests on the ground slightly behind the throwing side foot and is very much like the out-field blocking position.

Neither catching stance is a natural position, and there is a trade-off between comfort and mobility. To take advantage of the mobility offered by the squatting stance and the comfort of the kneeling stance, have your players alternate between these positions. When the pitcher is getting set and the catcher presents a target, use the kneeling stance; then to catch pitches, shift into the squatting stance.

Coaching Points for the Catcher's Stance

1. Position catchers directly behind home plate.
2. The feet should be about hip-width apart.
3. Keep the legs in a front-to-back position.
4. Balance the body weight between both legs.
5. Keep the back straight and the rear down.

Receiving the Pitch

To receive pitches, the catcher needs to be set before the pitch is thrown. Demonstrate how to set-up holding the mitt in a fingers-up position and present a steady target for the pitcher, as illustrated in Figure 9-3. Because the catcher's mitt is so large, players may have difficulty holding a steady target with one hand, so be sure to show them how to place the free hand behind the mitt for additional support.

Fig. 9-2

CATCHER'S KNEELING STANCE

Fig. 9-3

As with all catches, receiving the pitch concludes with trapping the ball. The best way to trap the ball is to cushion the catch by letting the pitch softly punch back the mitt, by sliding the free hand around the mitt, and by grasping the ball. This can be tricky. Stress to your players it is most important to use the free hand for support and then to trap the ball. Never place the free hand in front of the mitt before the ball is in the glove.

Two protection reactions catchers need to overcome are (a) closing the eyes, and (b) turning the head. These reactions are natural protection devices that can be overcome only by catching pitches in competitive situations during each practice. To protect the body, catchers must wear a face mask with a throat protector, a chest protector, and leg guards. (It is recommended that boys also wear a cup.) However, this equipment will only protect the catcher if the head is held steady, facing the pitch (see Figure 9-4). If the catcher turns to the side, the head, neck, back, and legs will be exposed and could be injured.

Fig. 9-4

Coaching Points for Receiving the Pitch

1. Extend the glove arm with elbow slightly bent.
2. Place the throwing hand behind the mitt.
3. Watch the ball.
4. Keep the head and body facing the pitch.

Blocking Pitches

Low pitches present a special problem, because to catch them, the mitt must be turned around so that the fingers point down, as shown in Figure 9-5. But, not all low pitches can be caught; some can only be blocked. Pitches thrown in the dirt are difficult to see and more difficult to catch. To block these pitches, show your players how to drop onto both knees, place the mitt between the legs, and use the entire body to block the ball (see Figure 9-6). Remember the principal rule of fielding: *keep the ball in front.*

Pitches thrown off to the side are also difficult to catch, and reaching out with the mitt is not an effective way to stop the ball. Study Figures 9-7 and 9-8 and show your players how to move the feet, shift to the side quickly, and get the

Fig. 9-5

Fig. 9-6

Fig. 9-7

Fig. 9-8

body in front of the ball. The Shift Drill (9.1) is a very versatile drill for catchers that can be used to practice blocking low pitches and pitches thrown to the side.

Coaching Points for Blocking the Pitch

1. Watch the ball.
2. Drop onto the knees or shift the body.
3. Place the mitt down to block the ball.
4. Keep the ball in front.

Teaching Progression for Catching Fast Pitches

1. Teach the proper stance.
2. Demonstrate how to hold and use the mitt.
3. Practice catching and throwing easy pitches.
4. Gradually progress to catching faster pitches.
5. Teach how to block pitches.
6. Practice catching in game situations.

Catching Slow Pitches

Catching in slow-pitch softball is quite different than in fast-pitch softball: Slow-pitch softball does not allow bunting or stealing; the ball is dead after each called ball or strike; and the slow, arching pitch is not as dangerous as a fast, straight pitch. Therefore, it is not crucial that catchers in slow-pitch block pitches or wear much protective equipment. (A catcher's mask with throat protector is recommended.) However, it is still important for the catcher to give the pitcher a target. As illustrated in Figure 9-9, position the slow-pitch catcher farther behind home plate than the catcher in fast-pitch softball. From this position, he or she can hold out the glove as a target, watch the ball bounce, and be well away from the bat and most foul balls.

Fig. 9-9

Catching Drills

(9.1) Shift Drill

Age: 9 years and up

Purpose: To help catchers learn to shift on pitches in the dirt

Equipment: Full catcher's equipment, sometimes no equipment

Procedure: Begin the drill by having catchers block imaginary pitches that come at them in the dirt, directly at their feet and to either side. Initially, they should do this without equipment. When they feel comfortable moving up, down, and to the side, have them practice moving after imaginary pitches wearing their equipment. Once your catchers are able to move well while wearing their equipment, gradually progress from throwing them easy ground balls to throwing actual pitches.

Softball
Planning Guide

Now that you know how to teach softball skills, you are probably eager to begin practice sessions. But unless you know how to design and conduct practices, your enthusiasm could end in frustration. To conduct an effective practice requires careful planning. Take the time to study this Planning Guide section of *Coaching Softball Effectively* and you will find practices more beneficial and enjoyable for your players—and you.

In this Planning Guide you will find information on how to explain the game of softball; how to develop long term seasonal plans and daily practice plans; how to create an environment that will enhance the presentation and practice of softball skills; and how to evaluate your players' skills and your coaching practices. Just as the Coaching Guide was a practical explanation of how to teach softball skills, this Planning Guide is a practical explanation of how to conduct effective practices.

In chapter 12 you will find seasonal plans and daily practice plans for three age groups: 6 to 8 years, 9 to 12 years, and 13 to 15 years. These plans include all of the skills needed to play softball. The skills are taught at a slower rate for younger, less skilled players and at a faster rate for older, more mature players.

Part III:
Presenting the Game
to Your Players

Softball is such a popular American game that most young people generally understand some game procedures. For example, they probably know that pitchers try to pitch the ball, batters try to hit the ball, and fielders try to field the ball. Your players, however, may not understand some of the fundamental features of softball that are necessary for playing the game. This part of the Planning Guide presents a short history of softball and focuses on how you can explain the parts of the playing field, the role of the umpire, balls and strikes, and the other rules that govern softball game play.

Chapter 10: The History of Softball

As a softball coach, you will probably like to know how this very popular American game developed. Thus, we have prepared a condensed history, highlighting the evolution of America's most popular participant sport.

As the legend goes, on Thanksgiving Day, 1887, at the Farragut Boat Club in Chicago, some men were waiting around to hear the results of the Harvard-Yale football game. In fun, one man threw a boxing glove at another who hit it with a broomstick. This triggered an idea in the mind of George Hancock, one of the players. He used the laces of the boxing glove to tie it into a ball. The large, soft ball did not travel nearly as far as would a baseball and allowed the men to play a modified game of baseball indoors. Hancock continued to develop the game by codifying a set of rules and called the game *indoor baseball*.

Indoor baseball became popular throughout the gyms of Chicago during the winter when people could not play baseball outside. Its popularity continued in the spring when players discovered that indoor baseball was a great game to play in the empty lots of the city, and soon indoor baseball became *indoor-outdoor*.

Although Hancock and his friends may have been first to play the modified baseball game, they were not the only ones to develop a game that fit smaller confines. Lewis Rober, a member of the municipal fire department of Minneapolis, developed a similar game for the fire fighters to play during the winter months. Their game was called *kitten ball*.

Indoor-outdoor, kitten ball, diamond ball, mush ball, or any of the other early versions of softball were especially popular in the northern cities because players did not need as much space to play; thus, it was easily adapted for indoors. Even though the game was popular all over the country, no national organized structure existed, every city seeming to have its own version of the game. Then in 1926, the first efforts to standardize a set of rules were made by the National Recreation Congress. Nothing substantial resulted from the meeting except that Walter Hakanson of the Denver YMCA introduced the name *softball* for the sport. Within 4 or 5 years, softball became the standarized name, but varying sets of rules still existed.

Thus, when the first cross-regional tournament was held in Milwaukee in 1932, mass confusion was the result because the 40 participating teams used at least 12 different sets of rules for the game. This experience prompted Leo Fischer, another Chicagoan, to organize a conference in 1933 at the Chicago World's Fair. At this conference, members from all the regions met in an attempt to standardize the rules. The Amateur Softball Association (ASA) grew out of these initial meetings and still remains the national governing body for the sport.

Softball's popularity grew rapidly in the 1930s and '40s, and today it is the largest team-participation sport in the country. Over 26 million people of all ages play softball in the United States, its popularity increasing throughout the rest of the world as well. Since these beginnings, softball has grown to include approximately 5 million youngsters.

Traditionally a favored girls' sport, softball has become a great game for boys as well. The large ball and natural pitching motion make it easier for youngsters to learn and is potentially less harmful for their growing bodies. Softball is just as popular with adults. In fact, more adults play softball than baseball. There are thousands of softball teams for adults as compared to the relatively few recreational baseball teams.

The many types of softball is another advantage softball has over baseball. Fast-pitch softball is a popular competitive game, especially for high school and college-age women. Slow-pitch softball varies from a recreational game to one that can be highly competitive, and 16-inch softball is still played in many schools and recreation programs.

Chapter 11: The Game of Softball

Introducing Softball

One of your responsibilities is to teach players softball rules and regulations, some of which were explained in the Softball Coaching Guide. Because softball is such a popular game, your players will be familiar with some rules and terms, but playing competitive games requires more than a general understanding of some rules; players must understand each rule affecting softball game play. As an adult your experience and understanding of softball is much better than your players', so some of the following material may seem unnecessary. But remember, this chapter is not intended to teach you softball; it is intended to help you explain the game to beginning players whose first formal introduction to softball may be through you.

If you want to find out how complicated softball rules are, just look through a rule book: There are hundreds of rules and regulations covering a multitude of situations. Do not worry, however, about covering all the rules presented in a rule book; those specific situations are included to help umpires control the game, and some situations even confuse umpires. What your players need to know are the basic rules concerning the playing field, the equipment, the teams, and the game procedures. This chapter presents this information in two ways: (a) in simple explanations your players can easily understand, and (b) in a stimulating question-and-answer session which actively includes your players in the learning process.

The Playing Field

Explain to your players that softball is played on a field that is shaped like and called a *diamond*. This diamond shape is formed by the line extending from home plate to first base, and the line from home plate to third base (see Figure 11-1). These lines, called *foul lines*, extend beyond the bases to the outfield fence and form a *V* at home plate.

Fair and Foul Territory

Be sure your players know the difference between fair and foul by explaining that the area inside the foul lines is called *fair territory*, and the area outside the foul lines is called *foul territory*. Balls hit within fair territory are considered "live" and must be played. Balls hit in foul territory are also live but need *not* be played.

Beginning players could become confused when a ball is first hit into fair territory but then rolls into foul territory. Explain that a ball which rolls into foul territory is foul unless it passes first base or third base before it rolls into foul territory (see Figure 11-2).

Within the playing field are the bases, home plate, and pitching rubber. Your players should understand that a ball which touches the bases, home plate, or pitching rubber is considered live and in fair territory, even if it hits a base and then bounces into foul territory.

Fig. 11-1

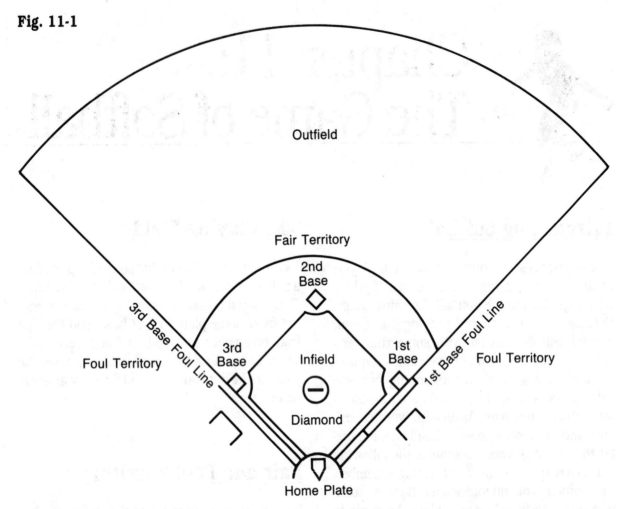

Offense and Defense

The terms *offense* and *defense* refer to the role of each team during a game. The offense is the team up to bat, and the runners and batters are the offensive players. The team out in the field is the defensive team, and the players who field the ball are the defensive players. When the defensive team is able to put out three offensive players, the offensive team and defensive team switch positions.

Although you understand the concept of an inning, it may be difficult to explain to your players. It will help your players to know that innings are like turns playing offense and defense. Each time one team has played both offense and defense, 1 inning has been played. Most youth league softball games last 5 innings. This means each team has 5 chances to bat and 5 chances to play the field.

Fig. 11-2

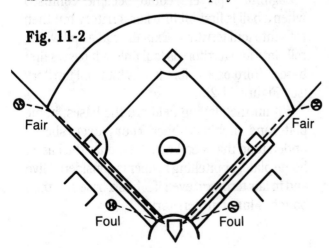

Offensive and Defensive Objectives

Softball is played by two teams, each composed of 9 players (10 for slow pitch). The objective

of the offensive team is to hit a ball and run counterclockwise around the bases and back to home plate. The objective of the defensive team is to stop the offensive team from scoring by making 3 outs. Explain to your players that (a) *runs* are scored when offensive players are able to move around all the bases and back to home plate; (b) an *out* is made when an offensive player is not able to advance; and (c) the winning team is the team with the most runs at the end of the game.

Balls and Strikes

Beginning players are interested in playing and having fun, so they will want to know how games begin. Tell your players games begin when a ball is pitched by a defensive player called the *pitcher*. This player pitches from a *pitching rubber* to an offensive player called the *batter* who stands in a *batting box* near home plate.

There are batting boxes on both sides of home plate, and batters can stand in either box. The ball is pitched when the pitcher and batter are ready to play. If the ball is pitched over the plate between the batter's knees and armpits, the ball is called a *strike*, and this area is called the *strike zone* (see Figure 11-3).

Batters can get strikes in several ways: first, when a batter does not hit a ball pitched in the strike zone; second, when the batter hits the ball into foul territory. This is called a *foul ball* and counts as a strike. The only time a foul ball does not count as a strike is when there are 2 strikes on a batter. And finally, a strike is called when a batter swings at the ball and misses. After 3 strikes, the batter is out, but after 4 balls, the batter is awarded first base.

Baserunning

Baserunning can be confusing to beginning players, but it need not be. The bases must be run in order from the batter's box to first, to sec-

Fig. 11-3

ond, and to third base, then back to home plate as shown in Figure 11-4. Bases are safe areas, so when a runner is touching a base, he or she cannot be put out; but when a runner is not touching a base, he or she can be put out.

Fig. 11-4

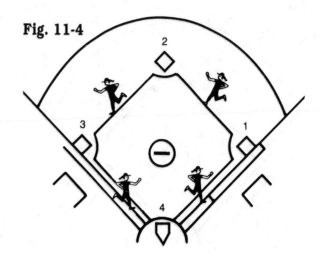

Base runners can also be *forced* to run to another base. For example, when batters hit a ball, they must run to first base, and when they are on first base and a ball is hit, they must run to second base. Two runners cannot be on one base at the same time. It is important that your players understand force situations because the defense can put out runners forced to a base simply by tagging the base before the runner does.

Another part of baserunning your players should understand are the *base paths*. Explain that the base paths are the distances directly between the bases; if a straight line were drawn between the bases, this would be the *baseline* (see Figure 11-5). Runners can be called out if they run outside of the baseline to avoid being tagged with the ball.

Interference and Obstructions

Occasionally, base runners and fielders get in each other's way. Even though these situations are frustrating and are sometimes difficult to avoid, they will occur less often if players understand the rules about interference and obstructions.

Explain that defensive players cannot get in the way of the base runner unless they are fielding the ball or making an out. When a defensive player gets in the way of the base runner, it is called an *obstruction*, and the base runner is allowed to reach that base safely (see Figure 11-6).

Fig. 11-5

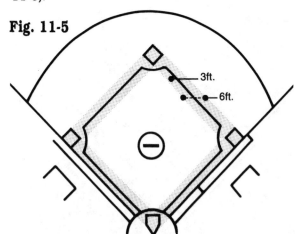

Fig. 11-6

Interference is called when runners get in the way of a defensive player fielding the ball or making an out (see Figure 11-7). The base runner who interferes with a defensive player will be called out; furthermore, if the umpire decides that the interference prevented the defense from putting out another base runner, then that base runner is also out.

The Infield Fly Rule

A rule which is difficult for young players to understand is the *infield fly rule*, which prevents the defensive team from making 2 outs by dropping an easy fly ball. Here is how the infield fly rule works: When runners are on first base and second base, or the bases are *loaded* (a runner on each base) with less than 2 outs, and an easy fly ball is hit to the infield, the umpire will call "infield fly, batter is out." When an infield fly is called, the batter is automatically out, and the

Fig. 11-7

other base runners are not forced to the next base; this prevents the defensive team from letting the fly ball drop to the ground and forcing out runners at two bases (getting a *double play*).

Umpires

Umpires are the ultimate authority on rules and enforcement of the rules. The umpires are often seen as bad guys by players, coaches, and spectators because they are usually only noticed when they make a close call. Umpires decide whether a pitch is a strike or ball, whether a hit is fair or foul, and whether a runner is safe or out. Like all people, umpires will make mistakes from time to time. What is important is how you as a coach react when you think the umpire made a mistake. Remember, you need to be a role model for your players. The rules state that no one should question the judgment of the umpire. But, if you think a rule was not properly enforced or is interpreted differently from the way you understand the rule, you are allowed to question the umpire. When you do question the umpire, ask for *time out* and stay calm. Do not interrupt the game by screaming and arguing.

Treat Umpires With Respect

Most likely your umpires are parents, other coaches, or players who also want to help young players have the opportunity to play softball. They, like you, are volunteers and not professionals. They are trying to make the game more pleasant for you and your players. Help them by responding calmly and reasonably.

Know the Rules

As a youth softball coach, you should understand the rules to softball game play. If you do not have a rule book, ask your league for one, or refer to the Rules of the Amateur Softball Association located in Appendix A.

Presenting the Rules and Procedures

A useful method to explain or to review the rules and procedures of softball play is to have a question-and-answer session while on a softball field or while watching a softball game. Either situation provides active participation for your players, and learning will be greatly enhanced by becoming involved with a demonstration rather than by simply sitting and listening. For example, if you asked where the players are positioned, you could move players to each position.

Be creative and appeal positively to each player. Laughing or poking fun at players may hurt their self-confidence and make them hesitant to participate in the activity. If players do not know the answer to a question, explain the answer and, if possible, demonstrate it for them.

Suggested Questions

The following questions have been designed to help you explain softball game play. They are divided into four major areas of softball: (a) the field, (b) the equipment, (c) the teams, and (d) game play. Ask each question and discuss the answer thoroughly before moving on. To prevent your players from becoming confused, these questions have been arranged in a purposeful progression, each question leading to the next.

Remember, the questions have not been designed to test your knowledge of softball, but to help you explain softball to *beginning* softball players. If you wish to use other questions or another method to explain the game, feel free to do so. As a coach, you need to decide which method will help you best explain the game to your players at their level of understanding.

The Field

1. Q: What is another name for the softball field?
   A: A softball *diamond*.

2. Q: Why is the field called a diamond?
   A: The field has the shape of a diamond.
3. Q. How many bases are used in softball?
   A: Three bases and one home plate are used in softball.
4. Q: Where are the bases located?
   A: First base is located down the right side of the field; third base is located down the left side of the field; and second base is located in between first base and third base. The bases are placed equal distances away from each other.
5. Q: Where are the *foul lines*?
   A: There are two foul lines. One foul line extends from home plate to first base and out to right field; the other foul line extends from home plate to third base and out to left field.
6. Q: What is the difference between *fair* territory and *foul* territory?
   A: Fair territory is the field *inside* the foul lines. Foul territory is the field outside the foul lines.
7. Q: Where is the *infield*?
   A: The infield is inside the foul lines—between home plate and the bases.
8. Q: Where is the *outfield*?
   A: The outfield is within the foul lines—between the infield and the outfield fence.
9. Q: What does *out of play* mean?
   A: Out of play means the ball is hit or thrown outside of the playing field. When a ball is out of play, base runners cannot advance or be put out.
10. Q: What are the *dugouts*?
    A: The dugouts are where the teams sit and are located along the first base and third base sides of the playing field.
11. Q: Are the dugouts in fair territory, foul territory, or out of play?
    A: The dugouts are out of play.

Equipment

1. Q: What are the three parts to the bat?
   A: The bat has a barrel, a knob, and a han-

dle. (Explain these parts and their uses to your players.)

2. Q: Why are gloves used?
   A: Gloves are used to help catch the ball.
3. Q: What is the difference between a *glove* and a *mitt*?
   A: Gloves are not as large as mitts.
4. Q: Which players can wear a mitt?
   A: Catchers and first basemen are the only players who can wear mitts.
5. Q: What equipment does a catcher wear?
   A: The catcher wears a facemask, a throat protector, a chest protector, a mitt, and leg protectors.
6. Q: What type of shoes are players allowed to wear?
   A: Players are allowed to wear tennis shoes, running shoes, or rubber-studded cleats. Players cannot wear shoes with metal cleats.

The Teams

1. Q: How many players can play for each team?
   A: Each team can play 9 players at a time for fast-pitch and 10 players for slow-pitch.
2. Q: What does *offense* mean?
   A: Offense means a team tries to hit the ball, to run the bases, and to score runs.
3. Q: Where are the offensive players positioned?
   A: The offensive players are either up to bat or on the bases.
4. Q: What does *defense* mean?
   A: Defense means a team tries to prevent the offensive team from hitting the ball, from running the bases, and from scoring runs. The defense tries to "put out" the offensive team.
5. Q: Where are the defensive players positioned?
   A: The defensive players are the catcher and pitcher; first, second, and third basemen; the right, center, and left fielders; and the shortstop. (Move your players to these positions)

Game Play

General

1. Q: How is a softball game started?
   A: Softball games begin when a ball is pitched. The pitcher begins each play by pitching a ball to a batter.

2. Q: What happens when a batter hits the ball?
   A: The batter tries to run the bases.

3. Q: What is an *umpire*?
   A: Umpires are the officials who control the game, call balls and strikes, call players out and safe, and make sure the game is played properly. Umpires are on the field to help you have fun playing softball.

4. Q: What does a *live ball* mean?
   A: Play is live when the umpire calls "Play ball," and the game is in progress.

5. Q: What does a *dead ball* mean?
   A: Play is dead when an umpire calls "Time-out!" Play is also dead when a ball is hit foul or out of play. A dead ball means the game is not in progress, so runners cannot advance or be put out.

6. Q: What is an *out*?
   A: Players are out when they are unable to hit a ball or reach a base safely. When players are out, they must leave the field until their next turn at bat.

7. Q: What is a *tag-out*?
   A: A tag-out is touching the base runner with the ball when the runner is not on a base.

8. Q: What is a *force-out*?
   A: A force-out is touching a base while holding the ball before the runner reaches the base. Force-outs can be made only when a runner *must* run to a base.

9. Q: What is a *fly-out*?
   A: A fly-out is catching a ball on the fly or before it touches any part of the field. Batters are automatically "out" when a fly ball is caught.

10. Q: What is an *inning*?
    A: An inning is each team's opportunity to bat and to play the field. The offensive team gets to bat until 3 outs are made, then the defensive team gets to bat.

11. Q: How many innings are in each game?
    A: This answer will depend on your league rules. Each game usually has 7 innings. However, many youth leagues play 5-inning games.

Pitching and Batting

1. Q: Are balls pitched *underhand* or *overhand*?
   A: Balls are pitched underhand.

2. Q: Where do batters stand?
   A: Batters stand in the *batter's box*. A batter's box is located to the left- and right-hand side of home plate. (Move two players to the batter's box.)

3. Q: Can batters step out of the batter's box to hit a ball?
   A: No! Batters are called out if they step outside of the batter's box to hit a ball.

4. Q: What is the *strike zone*?
   A: The strike zone begins at a batter's knees and extends to the batter's armpits.

5. Q: What is a *strike*?
   A: A strike is (a) a ball that has crossed home plate within the strike zone, (b) a swing and miss, and (c) a foul ball.

6. Q: How many strikes can a batter get before being called out?
   A: Batters are called out after they have made 3 strikes.

7. Q: What is a *ball*?
   A: A ball is a pitch that does not cross the strike zone.

8. Q: How many balls can a batter get before going to first base?
   A: Batters can go to first base after they have been pitched 4 balls.

9. Q: Can pitchers *fake* a pitch?
   A: No! Pitchers must pitch to the batter. A fake is ruled an illegal pitch and will be called a ball.

Baserunning and Fielding

1. Q: Are the bases run in any particular order?

   A: Yes! The bases must be run in the following order: first base to second base to third base to home plate. When runners want to return to a base, they must run the bases in reverse order: from third to second to first. Runners cannot cut across the field.

2. Q: What is a *baseline*?

   A: The baseline is the path directly between two bases. Base runners must run along this baseline.

3. Q: What happens if base runners run outside of the baseline to avoid being tagged out?

   A: Base runners are called out when they run outside of the baseline to avoid being tagged out.

4. Q: Which base can be *overrun*?

   A: Base runners can run past (overrun) first base without being tagged out.

5. Q: Why do runners have to touch a base?

   A: Bases are considered safe territory. Base runners cannot be called out while they are touching a base.

6. Q: Can base runners leave a base at any time?

   A: No! Base runners must stay on base until the ball is pitched. If base runners leave the base early, they will be called out.

7. Q: What must base runners do if a fly ball is caught?

   A: Base runners cannot leave a base until a fly ball is caught. If they leave the base early, they must return and touch that base before they can run to the next base. This is called *tagging up*.

8. Q: What is *interference*?

   A: Base runners cannot hinder a fielder from catching a ball or from making a play. When base runners hinder a fielder, it is called interference, and the base runner will be out.

9. Q: What is *obstruction*?

   A: Obstruction is blocking a base runner. When this happens, the base runner is able to move to the next base.

10. Q: Why are there *base coaches*?

    A: Base coaches are used to help base runners run the bases. One base coach is at first base and one base coach is at third base. Base coaches tell runners to stop at a base or to run to another base.

Game Play Drills

The Playing Rules Drill (11.1) can be used to teach your players the rules and game play of softball. We suggest you modify this drill to meet the needs of your team and to correspond with the rules of your softball league. Conduct the Playing Rules Drill as indicated below:

(11.1) Playing Rules Drill

Age: 9 years and up

Purpose: To teach players the rules of softball using practical and meaningful situations. This drill can be used to explain all playing rules.

Equipment: Balls, bats, one set of bases

Procedure: Select the rules you wish to teach prior to beginning this drill. Once the rules have been selected, explain the rule to the players simply and clearly. Then set up practical situations to illustrate the rules. For example: "When a ball is touched in foul territory before it reaches first or third base, the ball is foul. This means the batter and any base runners cannot run the bases." To illustrate this rule, have your players line up near one of the foul lines while you roll balls fair and foul. Let your players call out which balls are fair and which are foul.

Part IV: Planning Your Practice Sessions

Practice sessions are the most important part of the softball season. These are the times once or twice a week your players receive detailed instruction, practice their skills, develop new friendships with their teammates, and hopefully, have fun playing softball. Your preparation for each practice is vital to the success of every practice session. Conducting effective practices does not just happen but requires an *understanding* of softball skills, of how to teach beginning softball players, and of how to develop practice plans. Just as a highly skilled athlete who has practiced hard for many years makes difficult plays appear easy, careful planning will ensure that each practice is fun, effective, and easy to conduct.

If you are like most volunteer coaches, you probably have a full-time job, a home to care for, children to raise, and bills to pay. When you do have time to think about coaching a softball team, you probably do not have the 2 or 3 hours required to develop next week's practice plans let alone a plan for teaching skills throughout the season. We understand these time commitments, but we still want you to have carefully planned practice sessions. That is why we have included a set of seasonal plans and practice plans for you, fully developed and ready for you to use. These plans incorporate the coaching points, teaching progressions, and drills presented in the Softball Coaching Guide and can be modified to meet the specific needs of your team.

Also included in Part IV are suggestions for modifying the game of softball for younger players and what is necessary to prepare for each game.

Even with the best planning, not every practice will be trouble-free. You will need to resolve disputes, punish and reward players, and adjust practices according to the weather and field conditions. All of this valuable information, contained in the ACEP Level 1 coaching book *Coaching Young Athletes*, will help you be a more effective coach.

Chapter 12: Instructional Schedules and Practice Plans

Grouping Players

It is important you recognize that young people of the same age will not be of equal skill or physical maturation. Some 10-year-olds may be small, uncoordinated, and unable to participate effectively in a structured environment such as a controlled practice. Other 10-year-olds will be much larger, better skilled, and eager to be instructed as to what they should do in practice.

Consequently, it is not always fair to place young people who are the same age in the same leagues. Youngsters will benefit more by working with other children similar in size and skill, than with players who are similar in age. If it is at all possible, we highly recommend that you group young people according to size and skill, not age.

Suggested Game Modifications

As you read in chapter 10, "The History of Softball," this is a game created by and for adults. The distances between bases and between pitching rubber and home plate were created for adults. Also, the hitting and pitching skills, which often are not always easy for many adults, are especially difficult for young players. There-

fore, the game should be modified based upon the size and skill of the players.

We consulted with several youth leagues and national organizations to determine if certain modifications could help young, beginning players have more fun playing softball. After this, we considered the maturational development and skill levels of children between 6 years (less mature) and 15 years (more mature). The following game modifications were then developed to help young, beginning players develop softball skills and still have fun playing softball. We encourage you to study these rule modifications and use them in your league.

Age	Modifications
5-7	Bases: 45 ft apart. Pitching position: 30 ft from home plate; pitcher only has fielding responsibilities. Batting: Use a batting tee. Everyone bats once each inning in a 4-inning game. Baserunning: No stealing.
8-9	Bases: 50 ft apart. Pitching: 30 ft from home plate; offensive coaches pitch to their batters. Batting: No walks allowed; no bunting. Baserunning: No stealing.
10-12	Bases: 55 ft apart. Pitching: 36 ft from home plate; opposing pitcher pitches.

13-15   Bases: 60 ft apart.
         Pitching: 42 ft from home plate.

Instructional Schedules for Teaching and Refining Skills

You will need to develop a seasonal plan to teach softball skills effectively and to follow the teaching progressions presented in the Softball Coaching Guide. A *seasonal plan* is an overview of what will be accomplished during the season.

Developing seasonal plans will help you determine your team's status at the beginning of a season as well as evaluate your team's progress at various points throughout the season.

A good seasonal plan teaches fundamental skills and then progresses to more advanced skills. For instance, you would want to teach the batting grip before you teach how to swing the bat. Similarly, you would not want to teach your players positional coverage and responsibilities before you teach them how to wear and use their gloves properly.

4-Week Instructional Schedule for Youth Softball Ages 6-8

Goal: To help players learn and practice individual and team skills needed to play a regulation game after 4 weeks.

T(10): Teach and practice the skill initially in 10 min.
P(10): Review and practice the skill for 10 min.

*: These skills are practiced during the drills

Skills	Week 1		Week 2		Week 3		Week 4		Time in Minutes
	Day 1	Day 2	Day 3	Day 4	Day 5	Day 6	Day 7	Day 8	
Warm-up Exercises	T(5)	P(5)	P(5)	P(5)	P(5)	P(5)	P(5)	P(5)	40
Cool-down Exercises	T(5)	P(5)	P(5)	P(5)	P(5)	P(5)	P(5)	P(5)	40
Throwing/Catching									
Throwing motion	T(10)	*	*		*	*		*	10
Catching throws	T(10)	*	*		*	*		*	10
Skip and throw				T(10)	*	*		*	10
Drills		P(10)	P(10)		P(10)	P(5)		P(5)	40
Fielding									
Ground balls	T(15)	*	*			*	*	*	15
Fly balls			T(5)				*	*	5
Basket catch					T(10)		*	*	10
Drills		P(10)	P(10)			P(5)	P(10)	P(10)	45
Batting									
Swinging a bat	T(15)					*			15
Hitting off a tee		T(10)			*		*		10
Drills					P(10)	P(5)	P(10)		25
Baserunning									
First base		T(10)					*		10
Rounding bases			T(15)	*		*	*		15
Drills				P(10)		P(5)	P(10)		25
Positional Skills									
Coverage areas		T(10)		*			*	*	10
Backing up					T(10)		*	*	10
Drills				P(10)			P(10)	P(5)	25
Relaying the Ball					T(10)		P(10)		20
Game Play									
Softball rules			T(10)						10
Game play				T(10)					10
Practice games				P(10)		P(30)		P(30)	70

Three examples of how to use your seasonal plan outline to develop a series of practices are presented in this chapter. These plans cover the age ranges of (a) 6 to 8 years (less mature); (b) 9 to 12 years (moderately mature); and (c) 13 to 15 years (more mature). They also span a 4-week period with two practices each week for a total of eight practice sessions. Because these plans

4-Week Instructional Schedule for Youth Softball Ages 9-12

Goal: To help players learn and practice individual and team skills needed to play a regulation game after 4 weeks.

T(10): Teach and practice the skill initially for 10 min.
P(10): Review and practice the skill for 10 min.

*: These skills are practiced during the drills.

Skills	Week 1 Day 1	Day 2	Week 2 Day 3	Day 4	Week 3 Day 5	Day 6	Week 4 Day 7	Day 8	Time in Minutes
Throwing/Catching									
Throwing motion	T(10)	*							10
Catching throws	T(10)	*							10
Skip and throw				T(10)	*				10
Drills		P(10)			P(15)				25
Fielding									
Ground balls	T(10)	*	*		*	*	*	*	10
Fly balls		T(10)	*		*	*	*	*	10
Basket catch					T(15)	*	*	*	15
Drills			P(10)		P(20)	P(20)	P(15)	P(10)	75
Batting									
Swinging	T(10)	*		*	*		*		10
Bunting			T(10)	*			*		10
Drills		P(10)		P(10)	P(20)		P(15)		55
Baserunning									
First base		T(10)				*			10
Rounding bases			T(10)			*			10
Leaving/tag-ups				T(10)		*			10
Sliding							T(15)	*	15
Drills						P(20)		P(10)	30
Positional Skills									
Coverage areas	T(10)		*				*	*	10
Force/Tag-outs				T(10)			*	*	10
Backing up		T(10)	*				*	*	10
Drills			P(10)				P(15)	P(10)	35
Team Defense									
Relays/Cut-offs			T(10)				*		10
Bunt coverage					T(10)		*		10
Drills							P(15)		15
Game Play									
Softball rules	T(10)								10
Playing a game		T(10)							10
Playing strategy				T(10)					10
Practice games						P(40)		P(30)	70
The Slingshot Pitch			T(10)	P(10)	P(20)	P(20)		P(10)	70
Catching									
Catching pitches			T(10)	P(10)	P(10)	P(10)		P(10)	50
Blocking pitches						T(10)	*	*	10
Drills					T(10)	P(10)			20

4-Week Instructional Schedule for Youth Softball Ages 13 and Up

Goal: To help players learn and practice individual and team skills needed to play a regulation game after 4 weeks.

T(10): Teach skill for first time in 10 min.
P(10): Practice or drill the skill for 10 min.

*: These skill components are practiced during the drills for this playing category.

Skills	Week 1		Week 2		Week 3		Week 4		Time in Minutes
	Day 1	Day 2	Day 3	Day 4	Day 5	Day 6	Day 7	Day 8	
Throwing/Catching									
Throwing motion	T(10)	*	*						10
Catching throws	T(10)	*	*						10
Skip and throw			T(10)						10
Drills		P(10)		P(10)					20
Fielding									
Ground balls	T(10)					*	*	*	10
Fly balls		T(15)				*	*	*	15
Basket catch			T(15)			*	*	*	15
Drills					P(15)	P(15)	P(15)	P(20)	65
Batting									
Swinging a bat	T(10)	*				*	*		10
Bunting			T(15)			*	*		15
Placing hits					T(15)	*	*		15
Drills		P(10)				P(15)	P(P30)		55
Baserunning									
First base		T(10)				*		*	10
Rounding bases		T(10)				*		*	10
Leaving/tag-ups				T(15)		*		*	15
Sliding					T(15)	*		*	15
Drills						P(10)		P(10)	20
Positional Skills									
Coverage areas	T(10)		*		*				10
Force/Tag-outs				T(15)	*				15
Backing up		T(10)	*		*			*	10
Drills			P(10)		P(15)			P(10)	35
Team Defense									
Relays/Cut-offs			T(20)				*	*	20
Bunt coverage				T(10)			*	*	10
Double plays					T(20)		*	*	20
Drills							P(20)	P(10)	30
Game Play									
Softball rules	T(10)								10
Playing a game		T(15)							15
Playing strategy				T(15)					15
Practice games						P(40)		P(40)	80
Pitching									
Slingshot			T(15)	*	*	*	P(5)	*	20
Windmill							T(10)	*	10
Drills				P(15)	P(15)	P(15)		P(20)	65
Catching									
Catching pitches			T(15)	*	*	*	*	*	15
Blocking pitches						T(10)	*	*	10
Drills				P(15)	P(15)	P(10)	P(10)	P(20)	70

do not span an entire season, we have called them *instructional schedules* rather than seasonal plans.

These instructional schedules can be used in their present form, but they are intended to serve as general guides rather than as strict plans. If you find your players require more or less time to learn and to refine these skills, then you should adjust the presentation and practice times to meet the needs of your players. After the first 4 weeks of your season, use the format of the instructional schedules to develop additional long-term plans. By taking the time to study and use these instructional schedules, developing additional schedules will take far less time and will be a breeze to use.

Daily Practice Plans

The following daily practice plans correspond with the instructional schedules: There are eight practice sessions covering 4 weeks of the season. One set of plans is written for less mature players (about 6 to 8 years); the second set is for moderately mature players (about 9 to 12 years); and the third set is for more mature players (about 13 to 15 years). While these plans can be used without any changes, they will not be perfect for every team. When you modify these practice plans, be receptive to the input of your assistant coaches and your players. Assistant coaches may be able to observe some things you cannot, and your players will soon know which skills they need to practice and the drills which they enjoy.

The Practice Plan Format

Each practice plan has been designed to be taken onto the practice field and specifies the following:

- The amount of time needed for each practice
- The activities focused on during each practice
- The organization needed to conduct drills
- Coaching points to teach your players better

First, an overview of the entire practice is presented: The number of the practice, total practice time, instructional goals, drills, and equipment are included in this overview. The actual practice plan follows with time divisions, activities, organization, and coaching points specified.

The Component/Time column specifies: (a) whether the skill is to be taught or practiced, (b) the length in minutes for the activity, and (c) the elapsed practice time through that activity. The Activity/Drills column indicates the skill activities to be taught or practiced and the recommended drills for practicing those skills. Points for keeping everyone active and organized are included in the Organization column. Finally, hints to help you better teach and correct skills are found in the column labeled Coaching Points.

To obtain the best results from every practice, each plan includes the following components from the ACEP Level 1 book *Coaching Young Athletes*:

- Warming up
- Practicing previously taught skills
- Teaching and practicing new skills
- Practicing in game-like situations
- Cooling down
- Evaluating practice

These components need not be in this order, but they should be a part of each practice session. For example, teaching and practicing new skills is more important for the first few sessions than reviewing previously taught skills. Later in the season, reviewing previously taught skills and practicing in game-like situations is more important than teaching new skills. But, your players will need to warm-up, cool-down, and practice in game-like situations each practice.

Using the Drills

Every drill included in the practice plans can be found in the Drills section of each chapter in this book. The number at the end of each drill indicates the chapter in which the drill can be found and the number it is listed under in that chapter. For example, The Practice Game Drill is Number 8.14. This means it is located in chapter 8 and is the 14th drill listed in that chapter.

Practice Plan 1

Instructional Goals
Teach warm-up and cool-down exercises. Teach fundamentals of throwing, catching, fielding ground balls, and batting from a tee.

Equipment
Balls, bats, batting tees
For the coach: Player roster, practice plans, first-aid kit

Drills
Throwing—Ball Grip Drill; Flick the Ball Drill
Catching—Players pair up, throw and catch
Fielding—Fielding Position Drill; Fielding Ground Balls Drill
Batting—Swinging the Bat Drill

Component/Time	Activity/Drills	Organization	Coaching Points
Introduction 5 min	Meet players; check the roster.	Bring the team together.	Introduce the coaches. State your goals and expectations.
Warm-up 5 min (10 min)	Stretch, jog, and throw	Organize the team in a circle. Demonstrate from inside the circle.	Stretch slowly; do not bounce. Jog; do not run hard. Throw from a moderate distance.
Teach 20 min (30 min)	Throwing and Catching Ball Grip Drill Flick the Ball Drill Throw and catch	Bring the team together. Pair up players for drills. Pairs stand apart a moderate distance.	Demonstrate the grip, step, arm-swing, and follow-through. Look at the target and follow through.
Teach 15 min (45 min)	Batting Swing the Bat Drill	Bring the team together. Pair up players for drills. Spread apart and alternate players swinging with and without bats.	Demonstrate the grip, stance, stride, and armswing. Stress watching the ball and following through.
Teach 15 min (60 min)	Fielding Ground Balls Fielding Position Fielding Ground Balls Drill	Bring the team together. Pair up players for drills. Pairs stand apart a moderate distance.	Demonstrate the stance and glove position. Stress watching the ball and trapping the ball.
Teach/Cool-down 5 min (65 min)	Easy jogging, throwing, and stretching	Pair up for throws. Jog as a group. Stretch in a group circle.	Do not run hard. Throw easy. Stretch slowly; do not bounce.
Review/ Evaluation 5 min (70 min)	Review the skills taught today. Comment on practice performance.	Bring the team together. Watch your time; do not drag on.	Be positive and constructive. Compliment effort. Mention the time and place for next practice.

Practice Plan 2

Age: 6-8
Total time: 70 minutes

Instructional Goals
Review and practice the warm-up and cool-down exercises, throwing, fielding ground balls, and batting skills. Teach running to first base, and positional areas and responsibilities.

Equipment
Balls, bats, batting tees, complete set of bases, 2 first bases, batting helmets
For the coach: Player roster, practice plans, first-aid kit

Drills
Throwing/Catching—Flick the Ball Drill; Throw and catch
Fielding—Fielding Position Drill; Fielding Ground Balls Drill
Batting—Hitting Off a Tee Drill; Swinging the Bat Drill
Baserunning—Running to First Base Drill

Component/Time	Activity/Drills	Organization	Coaching Points
Introduction 5 min	Greet your players; check your roster. Tell players about today's practice.	Bring the team together.	Be prompt and enthusiastic. Briefly describe the practice.
Warm-up 5 min (10 min)	Easy stretching, jogging, and throwing	Organize the team in a circle. Lead stretching in the circle. Jog as a group. Pair up for throws.	Stretch slowly; do not bounce. Jog; do not run hard. Throw from a moderate distance.
Review/Practice 10 min (20 min)	Throwing/Catching Flick the Ball Drill Throw and Catch	Review in large group. Pair up players for drills. Pairs stand apart a moderate distance.	Emphasize the proper grip, stride, and arm swing. Correct skills as players practice.
Review/Practice 10 min (30 min)	Fielding Ground Balls Fielding Position Drill Fielding Ground Balls Drill	Review in large group. Pair up players for drills. Pairs stand apart a moderate distance.	Emphasize the proper body and glove position. Stress watching and trapping the ball.
Review/Practice 10 min (40 min)	Batting Hitting Off a Tee Drill Swinging a Bat Drill	Review in a large group. Divide team in half for drills. One group practices swings while the other hits off tees.	Emphasize the proper grip, stance, bat swing, and follow-through. Watch the ball and swing level.
Teach 10 min (50 min)	Baserunning Running Past First Base Drill	Teach in a large group. Set up 2 first bases. Divide team in half for the drill.	Have players run half the distance only. Stress running past the base and touching the front edge of the base.
Teach 10 min (60 min)	Positional coverage areas and responsibilities Throw balls to players at each position	Teach in a large group. Divide in half for practice. Rotate the players around each position.	Stress the coverage areas. Be sure each player fields at each position.
Cool-down 5 min (65 min)	Easy throwing, jogging, and stretching	Bring the team together. Pair up for throws. Jog as a group. Stretch in a circle.	Throw easy. Do not run fast. Stretch slowly; do not bounce.
Evaluation 5 min (70 min)	Review the practice	Discuss as a group.	Be positive and constructive. Compliment hustle and effort. Review areas that need work.

Practice Plan 3

Age: 6-8
Total time: 60 minutes

Instructional Goals
Review and practice throwing/catching and fielding ground balls. Teach fielding fly balls, running around the bases, and softball rules.

Equipment
Balls, 1 set of bases (2 first bases), rule book
For the coach: Player roster, practice plans, first-aid kit

Drills
Throwing/Catching—Ball Grip Drill; Throwing for Points Drill
Fielding—Fielding Ground Balls Drill; Judging Fly Balls Drill
Baserunning—Rounding First Base Drill
Softball Rules—Playing Rules Drill

Component/Time	Activity/Drills	Organization	Coaching Points
Introduction 5 min	Easy stretching, jogging, throwing	Stretch in a team circle. Jog as a group. Pair up for throws.	Check roster and discuss today's practice.
Practice 10 min (15 min)	Throwing/Catching Ball Grip Drill Throw and Catch	Pair up players. Players stand apart a moderate distance.	Emphasize striding toward the target, snapping the wrist, and the follow-through.
Teach/Practice 15 min (30 min)	Fielding Ground Balls Fielding Ground Balls Drill Judging Fly Balls Drill	Bring players together and teach in large group. Pair up players for drills.	Move to the ball. Watch the ball. Trap with free hand.
Teach 15 min (45 min)	Baserunning Rounding First Base Drill	Teach in a large group. Set up 2 first bases. Divide the team in half for the drill.	Swing to the outside, turn into the base, touch the inside corner of the base.
Teach 10 min (55 min)	Playing Rules Playing Rules Drill	Teach in a large group. Include players in the activity.	Be thorough, but do not drag on. Be positive and encourage player's participation.
Cool-down/ Evaluation 5 min (60 min)	Easy throwing, jogging, stretching	Pair up for throwing. Jog as a group. Stretch in a group circle.	Cool down easily. Evaluate the practice. Mention time and place for next practice.

Practice Plan 4

Age: 6-8
Total time: 60 minutes

Instructional Goals
Review the skill of running around the bases and the positional coverage areas. Teach the skip and throw and how to play a softball.

Equipment
Balls, bats, batting tees, helmets, 2 sets of bases, rule book
For the coach: Player roster, practice plans, first-aid kit

Drills
Baserunning—Running the Bases Drill
Positional Areas—Individual Position Drill
How to Play Softball—Playing Rules Drill
Skip and Throw—Step and Throw Drill

Component/Time	Activity/Drills	Organization	Coaching Points
Introduction/ Warm-up 5 min	Easy stretching, jogging, throwing a group. Pair up for throws.	Stretching in a team circle. Jog as a group. Pair up for throws.	Check roster and discuss today's practice.
Practice 10 min (15 min)	Baserunning Running the Bases Drill	Set up 2 diamonds. Divide the team in half.	Swing wide, turn into the base, touch the inside corner of the base.
Teach 10 min (25 min)	The Skip and Throw Step and Throw Drill	Teach the skill in a large group. Pair up players for the drill. Players stand apart a moderate distance.	Demonstrate the skip, the step, then the throw. Step at the target and follow through.
Practice 10 min (35 min)	Positional Areas Individual Position Drill	Divide the team in half. Have the groups practice on separate diamonds.	Stress making plays at each position. Back up other positions.
Teach 20 min (55 min)	How to Play Softball Playing Rules Drill Practice Game Drill	Conduct the Playing Rules Drill as a group. Divide the team in half for a 1-inning game.	Relate the rules to actual game play. Keep the game fun.
Cool-down/ Evaluation 5 min (60 min)	Easy throwing, jogging, stretching	Throw in pairs. Jog as a large group. Stretch in a group circle.	Evaluate the practice. Let them know you had fun today. Mention time and place for next practice.

Practice Plan 5

Age: 6-8
Total time: 60 minutes

Instructional Goals
Review the skip and throw. Practice batting off a tee. Teach the basket catch, backing up other players, and relaying the ball.

Equipment
Balls, bats, batting tees, 2 sets of bases
For the coach: Player roster, practice plans, first-aid kit

Drills
The Skip and Throw—Throwing for Points Drill
Batting—Hitting Off a Tee Drill
Fielding—Basket Catch Drill
Positional Skills—Reduced Playing Field Drill
Team Defense—Cut-off and Relay Drill

Component/Time	Activity/Drills	Organization	Coaching Points
Introduction/ Warm-up 5 min	Easy stretching, jogging, throwing	Lead stretches in a group circle. Jog as a group. Pair up to throw.	Check roster and discuss today's practice.
Review/Practice 10 min (15 min)	The Skip and Throw Throwing for Points Drill	Review in large group. Pair up players for Rhythm Drill.	Emphasize hopping onto and pushing off the back foot.
Practice 10 min (25 min)	Batting Hitting Off a Tee Drill	Pair up players. While one player bats, the other player watches for proper form.	Look for the batter striding straight ahead, swinging level, and following through.
Teach (10 min (35 min)	Fielding Fly Balls Basket Catch Drill	Teach in a large group. Divide team in half for practice.	Throw short fly balls. Palm of glove faces upward. Watch the ball; trap the ball.
Teach 10 min (45 min)	Backing Up Players Reduced Playing Field Drill	Teach in a large group. Divide team into groups for drill. Have players move to back up other fielders.	Position players 10 ft behind the fielder. Stand in the ready position.
Teach 10 min (55 min)	Relays Cut-off and Relay Drill	Teach in a large group. Divide into groups of 3-5 players for the drill.	Use the skip and throw. Throw accurately, not fast.
Cool-down/ Evaluation 5 min (60 min)	Easy throwing, jogging, stretching	Bring everyone together. Pair up for throwing. Jog as a group. Stretch in a group circle.	Provide feedback during cool-down. Praise effort and attention. A game is planned for next practice.

Practice Plan 6

Age: 6-8
Total time: 60 minutes

Instructional Goals
Practice all skills taught previously. Play a practice game. Prepare for game by throwing, catching, fielding, batting, and baserunning.

Equipment
Balls, bats, batting tees, 1 set of bases
For the coach: Player roster, practice plans, first-aid kit

Drills
Preparation for the Game—Throwing and catching; Ground Ball-Fly Ball Drill; Swinging the Bat Drill; Running the Bases Drill

Component/Time	Activity/Drills	Organization	Coaching Points
Introduction/ Warm-up 5 min	Easy stretching, jogging, throwing	Stretch in a group circle. Jog as a group. Pair up for throwing.	Check roster and discuss today's practice.
Practice 20 min (25 min)	Game Preparation Throwing and catching Ground Ball-Fly Ball Drill Swinging the Bat Drill Running the Bases Drill	Divide drills among coaches (2 drills for 2 coaches). Divide team in 4 groups. Rotate players through each drill.	Watch for proper form. Keep the players organized. Watch your time.
Practice 30 min (55 min)	Practice Game Practice Game Drill	Divide team in half. Players choose and play 2 positions.	Control the game. Give feedback, but let them play and have fun.
Cool-down/ Evaluation 5 min (60 min)	Easy throwing, jogging, stretching	Cool-down as a group.	Evaluate practice. Mention time and place for next practice. Be constructive and enthusiastic.

Practice Plan 7

Age: 6-8
Total time: 60 minutes

Instructional Goals
Review and practice the skills of fielding, batting, baserunning, positional play, and relaying the ball.

Equipment
Balls, bats, batting tees, 1 set of bases
For the coach: Player roster, practice plans, first-aid kit

Drills
Fielding—Ground Ball-Fly Ball Drill
Batting—Hitting Off a Tee Drill
Baserunning—Running the Bases Drill
Positional Play—Reduced Field Playing Drill
Relaying the Ball—Cut-off and Relay Drill

Component/Time	Activity/Drills	Organization	Coaching Points
Introduction Warm-up 5 min	Easy stretching, jogging, throwing	Stretch in a group circle. Jog as a group. Pair up for throwing.	Check the roster; review today's practice.
Practice 10 min (15 min)	Fielding Ground Ball-Fly Ball Drill	Divide the team in half. Have one group field while the other bats. Switch after 5 min.	Watch the ball; move to the ball; trap the ball in the glove.
Practice 10 min (25 min)	Batting Hitting Off a Tee Drill	Divide the team in half. Have one group bat while the other fields.	Use the proper stance. Stride into the hit; watch the ball; swing level; follow-through.
Practice 10 min (35 min)	Baserunning Running the Bases Drill	Divide the team in half. One group runs while the other plays positions. Switch after 10 min.	First base—Touch the front edge; run past the base; do not leap upon the base. Around the bases—Swing wide; turn into the base; touch the inside corner.
Practice 10 min (45 min)	Positional Play Reduced Playing Field Drill	Divide the team in half. Have one group practice positions while the other runs bases. Have players practice 2 positions.	Use proper fielding mechanics. Move on each play and back up other players.
Practice 10 min (55 min)	Relaying the Ball Cut-off and Relay Drill	Form groups of 3-5 players. Players stand apart a moderate distance.	Throw accurately, not fast. Use the skip and throw.
Cool-down/ Evaluation 5 min (60 min)	Easy throwing, jogging, stretching	Pair up for throws. Jog as a group. Stretch in a group circle.	Evaluate the practice. Be positive and constructive. Mention time and place for next practice.

Practice Plan 8

Age: 6-8
Total time: 60 minutes

Instructional Goals
Practice all skills taught previously by playing a practice game. Prepare for the game by throwing, fielding, and practicing positional play.

Equipment
Balls, bats, batting tees, 1 set of bases
For the coach: Player roster, practice plans, first-aid kit

Drills
Preparation for the Game—Ground Ball-Fly Ball Drill; Throwing for Points Drill; Individual Position Drill

Component/Time	Activity/Drills	Organization	Coaching Points
Introduction/ Warm-up 5 min	Easy stretching, jogging, throwing	Stretch in a group circle. Jog as a group. Pair up for throws.	Check the roster and discuss today's practice.
Practice 20 min (25 min)	Game Preparation Drills Ground Ball-Fly Ball Drill Individual Position Drill Throwing for Points Drill	Divide the team in 3 groups: One group fields, one practices positional play, one throws for points. Rotate players through the drills.	Fielding—Watch the ball; move to the ball; trap the ball. Positional Play—Play 2 positions; back up other players; throw accurately.
Practice 30 min (55 min)	Practice Game Practice Game Drill	Divide team in half. Set up the diamond.	Have fun. Compliment effort and hustle. Correct skills constructively.
Cool-down/ Evaluation 5 min (60 min)	Easy throwing, jogging, stretching	Pair up for throws. Jog as a group. Stretch in a group circle.	Let them know you had fun. Mention time and place of first game. Review skills to work on before the game.

Practice Plan 1

Age: 9-12
Total time: 80 minutes

Instructional Goals
Teach the fundamental skills of throwing, catching, fielding, and batting. Introduce players to playing positions and softball rules.

Equipment
Balls, bats, 1 set of bases, helmets
For the coach: Player roster, practice plans, first-aid kit

Drills
Throwing—Ball Grip Drill; Throwing Action Drill
Catching—Throwing and catching
Fielding—Fielding Position Drill; Fielding Ground Balls Drill
Batting—Simulating Swings Drill; Hitting Off a Tee Drill
Softball Rules—Playing Rules Drill

Component/Time	Activity/Drills	Organization	Coaching Points
Introduction 5 min	Introduce yourself and other coaches. Check the roster. Talk about how you will coach the team.	Bring the players together.	Be enthusiastic. Let them know you care about learning skills and about having fun.
Warm-up 5 min (10 min)	Easy stretching, jogging, throwing	Stretch in a group circle. Jog as a group. Pair up for throws and stand apart a moderate distance.	Lead and demonstrate stretches from inside the circle. Stretch slowly; do not bounce. Jog easily; do not race. Do not throw fast.
Teach/Practice 10 min (20 min)	Throwing Motion Ball Grip Drill Throwing Action Drill	Teach in a group. Pair up players for drills.	Emphasize the grip, arm swing, stride, and follow-through. Throw accurately.
Teach/Practice 10 min (30 min)	Catch Throws Throw and catch	Teach in a group. Pair up for drill.	Present how to wear and use the glove. Watch the ball; trap the ball.
Teach/Practice 10 min (40 min)	Fielding Fielding Position Drill Fielding Ground Balls	Teach in a group. Practice fielding position individually. Pair up for fielding ground balls.	Emphasize proper leg and hand position. Move to the ball; watch the ball; trap the ball.
Teach/Practice 10 min (50 min)	Batting Simulating Swings Drill Hitting Off a Tee Drill	Teach in a group. Pair up for drills. Players alternate swinging and watching for correct form. Spread apart and hit off a tee into fence or net.	Present proper grip, stance, stride, arm swing, and follow-through. Watch the ball.
Teach/Practice 10 min (60 min)	Positional Coverage Areas Move players through positions	Teach in a group. Rotate players through each position on the field.	Stress knowing the playing areas and the responsibilities of each position.
Teach 10 min (70 min)	Softball Game Rules Playing Rules Drill	Conduct question-and-answer session as a group. Involve your players in the presentation.	Explain the rules simply and clearly. Let your players show you their answers.
Teach/Cool-down 5 min (75 min)	Easy throwing, jogging, stretching	Pair up for throws. Jog as a group. Stretch in a group circle.	Throw easy, not fast. Jog easily; do not race. Stretch slowly; do not bounce.
Evaluation 5 min (80 min)	Review today's practice	Bring the players together.	Be positive and constructive; review the skills. Mention time and place for next practice.

Practice Plan 2

Age: 9-12
Total time: 80 minutes

Instructional Goals
Review and practice throwing, catching, and batting. Teach fielding fly balls, running to first base, back-up positions, and how to play a game.

Equipment
Balls, bats, batting tees, 2 sets of bases
For the coach: Player roster, practice plans, first-aid kit

Drills
Throwing/Catching—Throw and Catch; Throw and Step Back Drill
Batting—Hitting Off a Tee Drill or Simulating Swings Drill; Hitting Easy Pitches Drill
Fielding—Judging Fly Balls Drill
Baserunning—Running Past First Base Drill; Leaving the Batter's Box Drill
Backing-up—Backing-up Drill

Component/Time	Activity/Drills	Organization	Coaching Points
Introduction 5 min	Review the coaches' and players' names. Check the roster. Review your coaching philosophy.	Bring the players together.	Be enthusiastic. Let them know you care about learning skills and about having fun.
Review/Warm-up 5 min	Easy stretching, jogging, throwing	Stretch in a group circle. Jog as a group. Pair up for throws and stand apart a moderate distance.	Stretch slowly; do not bounce. Jog easily; do not race. Throw easy, not fast.
Review/Practice 10 min (20 min)	Throwing/Catching Throw and Catch Throw and Step Back Drill	Review throwing and catching fundamentals as a group. Pair up for drills.	Throwing—Proper grip, stride, follow-through. Catching—Glove control; watch and trap the ball.
Review/Practice 10 min (30 min)	Batting Hitting Off a Tee Drill, or Simulating Swings Drill Hitting Easy Pitches Drill	Review as a group. Pair up for drills. If tees are not available, divide team in half. Practice swings and let players hit easy pitches.	Proper grip; swing level; watch the ball; stride forward and follow-through.
Teach 10 min (40 min)	Fielding Fly Balls Judging Fly Balls Drill	Teach as a group. Divide team in half or drill.	Watch the ball; move to the ball; trap the ball.
Teach 10 min (50 min)	Baserunning Leaving the Batter's Box Drill Running Past First Base Drill	Teach as a group. Divide team in half for drill. Practice leaving the box drill first; then run past first base.	Run slowly at first, then faster. Touch the front edge of the base. Run beyond the base. Do not leap upon the base.
Teach 10 min (60 min)	Backing-up Backing-up Drill	Teach as a group. Divide team in half for drill.	Stand about 20 ft behind the fielder. Get in the ready position. Watch the ball.
Teach 10 min (70 min)	Playing a Game Explain how a game proceeds	Explain as a group. Use the discussion in *Softball Coaching Guide.*	Involve your players with the discussion.
Review/ Cool-down 5 min (75 min)	Easy throwing, jogging, stretching	Pair up for throwing. Jog as a group. Stretch in a group.	Throw easy, not fast. Jog easily; do not race. Stretch slowly; do not bounce.
Evaluation 5 min (80 min)	Review today's practice	Bring the players together.	Correct skills positively. Compliment effort and hustle. Mention time and place for next practice.

Practice Plan 3

Age: 9-12
Total time: 70 minutes

Instructional Goals
Review and practice fielding skills and backing up.
Teach bunting, rounding bases, relaying/cutting off throws, the slingshot pitch, and catching pitches.

Equipment
Balls, bats, 2 sets of bases, helmets
For the coach: Player roster, practice plans, first-aid kit

Drills
Fielding—Fielding Ground Balls Drill; Judging Fly Balls Drill
Backing up—Short Base Drill; Backing-up Drill
Bunting—Bunt Drill
Relays/Cut-off and Relay Drill
Pitching/Catching—Throwing and catching pitches
Baserunning—Rounding the Bases Drill

Component/Time	Activity/Drills	Organization	Coaching Points
Warm-up 5 min	Easy stretching, jogging, throwing	Stretch in a group circle. Jog as a group. Pair up for throws. Choose 2 players to lead warm-up.	Discuss practice and check roster during warm-up. Keep the warm-up easy.

Review/Practice
10 min (15 min)
	Fielding
	  Fielding Ground Balls Drill
	  Judging Fly Balls Drill
		Review fielding fly balls as a group. Divide team in half for drills.	Proper ready position. Watch the ball; move to the ball; trap the ball.

Teach 10 min (25 min)	Bunting Bunt Drill	Teach bunting as a group. Pair up players for drills.	Be sure to demonstrate from several angles. Square around; hold bat firm; try to catch the ball.
Teach 10 min (35 min)	Rounding the Bases Rounding the Bases Drill	Teach as a group. Divide team in half for drills.	Run only half the distance. Swing wide; turn into the base; and touch the inside corner.

Review/Practice
10 min (45 min)
	Positional Skills
	  Short Base Drill
	  Backing-up Drill
		Review coverage areas and backing-up as a group. Divide into small groups for drills.	Have players field 2 positions. Back up 10 ft behind fielder; watch the ball.

Teach 10 min (55 min)	Relays/Cut-offs Cut-off and Relay Drill	Teach as a large group. Divide into groups of 3-5 for drills.	Throw accurately, not fast. Watch the ball; trap the ball.
Teach 10 min (65 min)	Pitching/Catching Throwing and catching pitches	Teach as a group. Teach catching position first. Teach slingshot pitch second. Pair up for pitching/catching practice.	Catch—Keep back straight, feet spread apart; watch the ball. Pitching—Stride forward; swing the arm straight back and forward; slow backswing, fast downswing.
Cool-down/ Evaluation 5 min (70 min)	Easy throwing, jogging, stretching	Choose 2 players to lead the cool-down. Pair up for throws. Jog as a group. Stretch in a group circle.	Keep the cool-down easy; review practice during cool-down. Be constructive; mention time and place for next practice.

Practice Plan 4

Age: 9-12
Total time: 70 minutes

Instructional Goals
Review and practice hitting/bunting, pitching, and catching. Teach the skip and throw, leaving and tagging up bases, making force-outs and tag-outs, and softball playing strategy.

Equipment
Balls, bats, 2 sets of bases, helmets
For the coach: Player roster, practice plans, first-aid kit

Drills
Hitting/Bunting—Batting Practice
Pitching/Catching—Throwing and catching pitches
Skip and Throw—Step and Throw Drill
Baserunning—Leaving Bases Drill
Force-outs/Tag-outs—Force-out/Tag-out Drill
Playing Strategy—Playing Strategy Drill

Component/Time	Activity/Drills	Organization	Coaching Points
Warm-up 5 min	Easy stretching, jogging, throwing	Warm-up as a group. Choose 2 players to lead exercises.	Warm up easily.
Teach/Practice 10 min (15 min)	The Skip and Throw Step and Throw Drill	Teach in a group. Pair up players for the drill.	Use a short, low skip. Push off the back foot. Throw accurately, not fast.
Practice 10 min (25 min)	Batting Batting practice	Divide the team in half. Each half bats on separate diamonds. Players should swing and bunt.	Batting—Watch the ball; stride into the ball; swing level. Bunting—Turn square to the ball; hold the bat firm; try to catch the ball with the bat.
Teach/Practice 10 min (35 min)	Leaving/Tagging Up Leaving Bases Drill	Teach in a group. Divide the team in half for drills.	Do not leave before the pitcher releases the ball. Push off the base.
Teach/Practice 10 min (45 min)	Force-outs/Tag-outs Force-out/Tag-out Drill	Teach in a group. Divide the team in half for drills.	Force-outs—Move to the base; touch the base; catch the ball. Tag-outs—Stand behind the base; catch the ball; place the glove in front of the runner.
Teach/Practice 10 min (55 min)	Playing Strategy Playing Strategy Drill	Teach and drill as a group.	Involve players in the discussion. Stress the priority of each rule.
Review/Practice 10 min (65 min)	Pitching/Catching Hit the Mitt Drill	Review pitching and catching fundamentals as a team. Pair up for the drills. While one player pitches, the other catches.	Pitching—Stride straight ahead; swing arm straight back and forward; snap the wrist and step through. Catching—Provide a target; watch the ball; trap the ball.
Cool-down/ Evaluation 5 min (70 min)	Easy throwing, jogging, stretching	Choose 2 players to lead the cool-down. Review the practice during the cool-down.	Cool down easily. Positively correct errors; compliment effort. Mention time and place for next practice.

Practice Plan 5

Age: 9-12
Total time: 90 minutes

Instructional Goals
Review and practice the skip and throw, batting, fielding, pitching, and catching. Teach the basket catch and bunt coverage. Players select 2 positions for playing games.

Equipment
Balls, bats, 2 sets of bases, 2 sets of catching equipment, helmets
For the coach: Player roster, practice plans, first-aid kit

Drills
Skip and Throw—Skip and Throw Drill; Throw and Step Back Drill
Batting/Fielding—Batting/Fielding Drill
Pitching and Catching—Hit the Mitt Drill
Basket Catch—Basket Catch Drill
Bunt Coverage—Bunt Reaction Drill

Component/Time	Activity/Drills	Organization	Coaching Points
Warm-up 5 min	Easy stretching, jogging, throwing	Choose two players to lead the warm-up. Warm up as a group.	Warm up easily. Discuss today's practice.
Practice 15 min (20 min)	Skip and Throw Drill Throw and Step Back Drill	Pair up players a moderate distance. Combine these drills. Use the skip and throw. Step back after each catch; step forward after each miss.	Throw short and easy fly balls. Progress to more difficult flies. Watch the ball; trap the ball.
Teach 15 min (35 min)	The Basket Catch Basket Catch Drill	Teach as a group. Divide team in half for drills. Each half practices on a separate field.	Positively correct skills. Encourage good positional play.
Practice 20 min (55 min)	Batting/Fielding Batting/Fielding Drill	Divide the team in half; each half practices on separate diamonds. Each player chooses 2 positions. Pitchers and catchers move to next drill.	Throw pitches the batter can hit. Stress correct batting and fielding skills.
Practice 20 min (75 min)	Pitching/Catching Hit the Mitt Drill Shift Drill	While other players field and bat, the pitchers and catchers work together. Teach catchers to shift and block low pitches.	Show catchers how to wear the equipment. Stress accuracy, and catching pitches.
Teach/Practice 10 min (85 min)	Bunt Coverage Bunt Reaction Drill	Teach as a group. Divide team in half for the drills.	Charge the ball; call for the ball; back up players and bases.
Cool-down/ Evaluation 5 min (90 min)	Easy throwing, jogging, stretching	Choose 2 players to lead the cool-down as a group. Review the practice during the cool-down.	Cool down easily. Review skills that need improvement. Mention time and place for next practice.

Practice Plan 6

Age: 9-12
Total time: 70 minutes

Instructional Goals
Practice softball playing skills in a practice game. Review the skills of fielding, baserunning, and pitching. Teach catchers to block pitches.

Equipment
Balls, bats, 2 sets of bases, helmets, 2 sets of catching equipment
For the coach: Player roster, practice plans, first-aid kit

Drills
Fielding and Baserunning—Game Situation Drill
Pitching—Hit the Mitt Drill
Catching—Shift Drill

Component/Time	Activity/Drills	Organization	Coaching Points
Warm-up 5 min	Easy stretching, jogging, throwing	Choose 2 players to lead the warm-up. Warm up as a group.	Warm up easily. Discuss today's practice during the warm-up.
Practice 20 min (25 min)	Fielding and Baserunning Game Simulation Drill	Practice as a team, except for pitchers and catchers. Rotate players as fielders and runners.	Watch for good fielding technique. Correct poor baserunning technique.
Practice 20 min (25 min)	Pitching and Catching Hit the Mitt Drill Shift Drill	While other players field and run, pitchers and catchers practice together on another diamond.	Stress accuracy of the pitches, and catching the ball.
Practice 40 min (65 min)	Practice Game Practice Game Drill	Divide the team in half. Let each player field 2 positions. An inning ends when each player has batted.	Provide constructive advice for playing the game. Correct skills. Let them have fun.
Cool-down/ Evaluation 5 min (70 min)	Easy throwing, jogging, stretching	Choose 2 players to lead the exercises. Cool down as a group. Review the practice.	Tell them what to work on to play a game. Mention time and place of next practice.

Practice Plan 7

Age: 9-12
Total time: 70 minutes

Instructional Goals
Practice fielding skills, batting positional skills, and team defense. Teach the skill of sliding.

Equipment
Balls, bats, 2 sets of bases, catching equipment, materials to practice sliding
For the coach: Player roster, practice plans, first-aid kit

Drills
Fielding/Batting—Batting/Fielding Drill
Team Defense/Positional Skills—Relay and Cut-Off Drill; Individual Skills Drill
Baserunning—Practice sliding

Component/Time	Activity/Drills	Organization	Coaching Points
Warm-up 5 min	Easy stretching, jogging, throwing	Choose 2 players to lead the warm-up. Warm up as a group. Discuss today's practice.	Warm up easily.
Practice 15 min (20 min)	Fielding/Batting Batting/Fielding Drill	Practice as a group. Have each player practice 2 positions. Rotate batters and fielders.	Watch for positional play, backing up, and making outs. Correct batting and fielding mechanics.
Practice 15 min (35 min)	Positional Skills Individual Position Drill	Divide the team in half. Each group practices on separate diamonds. Each player practices 2 positions.	Correct positional play from the practice game.
Practice 15 min (50 min)	Team Defense Relay and Cut-off Drill Bunt Reaction Drill	Divide the team in half. Each group practices on separate diamonds.	Use the skip and throw for relays. Charge and call for bunts.
Teach 15 min (65 min)	Sliding Practice sliding	Teach and practice as a group. Wet down grass or plastic. (This is a fun drill.)	Bend the back leg; sit down on the thigh and rear; keep the hands held up.
Cool-down/ Evaluation 5 min (70 min)	Usual cool-down if players are dry; if wet, dry off and end practice.	Cool down as a group. Review today's practice.	Mention time and place for next practice.

Practice Plan 8

Age: 9-12
Total time: 70 minutes

Instructional Goals
Practice fielding, catching, and sliding, and prepare for a practice game by working on positional skills. Play a practice game.

Equipment
Balls, bats, 4 helmets, 2 sets of bases, 2 sets of catching equipment
For the coach: Player roster, practice plans, first-aid kit

Drills
Fielding—Outfield Ground Ball-Fly Ball Drill; Infield Teamwork Drill
Pitching/Catching—Pitching and catching practice
Baserunning—Sliding practice
Positional Skills—Individual Position Drill

Component/Time	Activity/Drills	Organization	Coaching Points
Warm-up 5 min	Easy stretching, jogging, throwing	Choose 2 players to lead the warm-up. Discuss today's practice.	Warm up easily.
Practice 10 min (15 min)	Fielding Outfield Ground Ball-Fly Ball Drill Infield Teamwork Drill	Divide the infielders and outfielders. Move outfielders to the outfield; move infielders to their positions. Pitchers and catchers practice together.	Outfield—Keep the ball in front; trap the ball. Infield—Move to the ball; back up; cover positional areas.
Practice 10 min (25 min)	Baserunning Sliding practice	Divide the team in 3 groups. Rotate groups to second, third, and home. Practice sliding at each base.	Keep the hands up; bend back leg and sit down on rear.
Practice 10 min (35 min)	Positional Skills Individual Position Drill	Bring the team together. Position 2 players at each position.	Emphasize positional coverage and hustle.
Practice 30 min (65 min)	Practice	Divide the team into 2 groups. Each inning is over when each player has batted.	Let players have fun. Provide advice for team play. Correct skill mechanics.
Cool-down/ Evaluation 5 min (70 min)	Easy throwing, jogging, stretching	Choose 2 players to lead the cool-down. Review today's practice.	Cool down easily. Mention skills to work on before the first game. Mention time and place of first game.

Practice Plan 1

Age: 13 and up
Total time: 80 minutes

Instructional Goals
Teach the fundamental skills of throwing, catching, fielding, and batting. Introduce the players to playing positions and softball rules.

Equipment
Balls, bats, 2 sets of bases, helmets
For the coach: Player roster, practice plans, first-aid kit

Drills
Throwing—Ball Grip Drill; Throwing Action Drill
Catching—Throwing and catching
Fielding—Fielding Position Drill; Fielding Ground Balls Drill
Batting—Swinging the Bat Drill
Softball Rules—Playing Rules Drill

Component/Time	Activity/Drills	Organization	Coaching Points
Introduction 5 min	Introduce yourself and other coaches. Check the roster. Talk about how you will coach the team.	Bring the players together.	Be enthusiastic. Let them know you care about learning skills and about having fun.
Warm-up 5 min (10 min)	Easy stretching, jogging, throwing	Stretch in a group circle. Jog as a group. Pair up for throws and stand apart a moderate distance.	Lead and demonstrate from inside the circle. Stretch slowly; do not bounce. Jog easily; do not race. Do not throw fast.
Teach/Practice 10 min (20 min)	Throwing Motion 　Ball Grip Drill 　Throwing Action Drill	Teach in a group. Pair up players for drills.	Emphasize the grip, arm swing, stride, and follow-through. Throw accurately.
Teach/Practice 10 min (30 min)	Catch Throws 　Throw and catch	Teach in a group. Pair up for drill.	Present how to wear and use the glove. Watch the ball; trap the ball.
Teach/Practice 10 min (40 min)	Fielding 　Fielding Position Drill 　Fielding Ground Balls Drill	Teach in a group. Practice fielding position individually. Pair up for fielding ground balls.	Emphasize proper leg and hand position. Move to the ball; watch the ball; trap the ball.
Teach/Practice 10 min (50 min)	Batting 　Simulating Swings Drill 　Hitting Off a Tee Drill	Teach in a group. Pair up for drills; players alternate swinging and watching for correct form. Spread apart and hit off a tee into fence or net.	Present proper grip, stance, stride, arm swing, and follow-through. Watch the ball.
Teach/Practice 10 min (60 min)	Positional Coverage Areas 　Move players through positions	Teach in a group. Rotate players through each position on the field.	Stress knowing the playing areas and the responsibilities of each position.
Teach 10 min (70 min)	Softball Game Rules 　Playing Rules Drill	Conduct question-and-answer session as a group. Involve your players in the activity.	Explain the rules simply and clearly. Let your players show you their answers.
Teach/Cool-down 5 min (75 min)	Easy throwing, jogging, stretching	Pair up for throws. Jog as a group. Stretch in a group circle. Lead stretches from inside the circle.	Throw easy, not fast. Jog easily; do not race. Stretch slowly; do not bounce.
Evaluation 5 min (80 min)	Review today's practice	Bring the players together.	Correct skills positively. Mention time and place for next practice.

Practice Plan 2

Age: 13 and up
Total time: 90 minutes

Instructional Goals
Review and practice throwing, catching, and batting. Teach fielding fly balls, running to first base, rounding the bases, backing up, and how to play a game.

Equipment
Balls, bats, 2 sets of bases
For the coach: Player roster, practice plans, first-aid kit

Drills
Throwing/Catching—Throw and catch; Throw and Step Back Drill
Batting—Hitting Easy Pitches Drill; Simulating Swings Drill
Fielding—Judging Fly Balls Drill
Baserunning—Leaving the Batter's Box Drill; Running Past First Base Drill
Backing Up—Backing Up Fielders Drill

Component/Time	Activity/Drills	Organization	Coaching Points
Introduction 5 min	Review the coaches' and players' names. Check the roster. Review your coaching philosophy.	Bring the players together.	Be enthusiastic. Let them know you care about learning skills and about having fun.
Review/Warm-up 5 min (10 min)	Easy stretching, jogging, throwing	Stretch in a group circle. Jog as a group. Pair up for throws and stand apart a moderate distance.	Lead and demonstrate stretches from inside the circle. Stretch slowly; do not bounce. Jog easily; do not race. Throw easy, not fast.
Review/Practice 10 min (20 min)	Throwing/Catching Throw and catch Throw and Step Back Drill	Review throwing and catching fundamentals as a group. Pair up for drills.	Throwing—Proper grip, stride, follow-through. Catching—Glove control; watch and trap the ball.
Review/Practice 10 min (30 min)	Batting Swinging the Bat Drill Hitting Easy Pitches Drill	Review as a group. Pair up for drills. Spread players apart a safe distance.	Proper grip; swing level; watch the ball; stride forward and follow through.
Teach 15 min (45 min)	Fielding Fly Balls Judging Fly Balls Drill	Teach as a group. Divide team in half for drill.	Watch the ball; move to the ball; trap the ball.
Teach 10 min (55 min)	Baserunning Leaving the Batter's Box Drill Running Past First Base Drill	Teach as a group. Divide team in half for drill. Practice the leaving the box drill first; then run past first base.	Run slowly at first, then faster. Touch the front edge of the base; run beyond the base. Do not leap upon the base.
Teach 10 min (65 min)	Backing Up Backing Up Drill	Teach as a group. Divide team in half for drill.	Stand about 20 ft behind the fielder. Get in the ready position. Watch the ball.
Teach 15 min (80 min)	Playing a Game Explain how a game proceeds	Explain as a group. Use the discussion in the *Softball Coaching Guide*.	Involve your players in the discussion.
Review/ Cool-down 5 min (85 min)	Easy throwing, jogging, stretching	Pair up for throwing. Jog as a group. Stretch in a group.	Throw easy, not fast. Jog easily; do not race. Stretch slowly; do not bounce.
Evaluation 5 min (90 min)	Review today's practice	Bring the players together.	Be positive; compliment effort and hustle. Provide constructive feedback.

Practice Plan 3

Age: 13 and up
Total time: 95 minutes

Instructional Goals
Review and practice backing up players. Teach the skip and throw, the basket catch, bunting, relays and cut-offs, and the slingshot pitch.

Equipment
Balls, bats, helmets
For the coach: Player roster, practice plans, first-aid kit

Drills
Throwing—Step and Throw Drill
Fielding—Basket Catch Drill
Batting—Bunt Drill
Relays/Cut-offs—Cut-off and Relay Drill
Backing Up—Backing-Up Drill
Pitching and Catching—Throwing and catching pitches

Component/Time	Activity/Drills	Organization	Coaching Points
Warm-up 5 min	Easy stretching, jogging, throwing	Stretch in a group. Jog as a group. Pair up for throws. Choose 2 players to lead warm-up.	Discuss practice and check the roster. Keep the warm-up easy.
Teach 10 min (15 min)	The Skip and Throw Step and Throw Drill	Teach as a group. Pair up for drills. Position players apart a moderate distance.	Hop low and short; push off the back foot; throw accurately.
Teach 15 min (30 min)	The Basket Catch Basket Catch Drill	Teach as a group. Divide the team in half for drill.	Watch the ball; move to the ball; trap the ball.
Teach 15 min (45 min)	Bunting Bunt Drill	Teach as a group. Pair up players for drill.	Watch the ball; square to the ball. Hold the bat firm; try to catch the ball.
Review/Practice 10 min (55 min)	Backing Up Backing-up Drill	Review as a group. Divide the team in half for the drill. Each half practices on separate diamonds.	Hustle! Back up 20 ft behind the fielder; watch the ball.
Teach 20 min (75 min)	Relays/Cut-offs Cut-off and Relay Drill	Teach as a group. Divide the team into groups of 3-5 for the drill.	Throw using the skip and throw. Throw accurately, not fast.
Teach 15 min (90 min)	Pitching/Catching Throwing and catching pitches	Teach the slingshot pitch and catching mechanics as a group. Pair up for practice.	Pitching—Swing the arm straight back and forward; step toward the target; snap the wrist and follow through. Catching—Watch the ball; trap the ball.
Cool-down/ Evaluation 5 min (95 min)	Easy throwing, jogging, stretching	Choose 2 players to lead the cool-down. Pair up for throws; jog as a group; stretch in a group circle.	Review the practice; be positive and constructive. They learned much today. Mention time and place for next practice.

Practice Plan 4

Age: 13 and up
Total time: 90 minutes

Instructional Goals
Practice throwing and catching and pitching the sling-shot pitch. Teach leaving and tagging up a base, force-outs and tag-outs, bunt coverage, and playing strategy.

Equipment
Balls, bats, 2 sets of bases
For the coach: Player roster, practice plans, first-aid kit

Drills
Throwing/Catching—Step and Throw Drill; Throw and Step Back Drill
Pitching/Catching—Throwing and catching pitches
Leaving and Tagging Up—Leaving Bases Drill
Force-outs/Tag-outs—Force-out-Tag-out Drill
Bunt Coverage—Bunt Reaction Drill
Playing Strategy—Playing Strategy Drill

Component/Time	Activity/Drills	Organization	Coaching Points
Warm-up 5 min	Easy stretching, jogging, throwing	Choose 2 players to lead the warm-up. Warm up as a group.	Keep the warm-up easy. Discuss today's practice.

Practice
10 min (15 min)
	Throwing/Catching
	  Step and Throw Drill
	  Throw and Step Back Drill
		Pair up for drills.	Throw accurately; push off the back leg; follow-through.

Teach 15 min (30 min)	Leaving/Tagging Up Leaving the Bases Drill	Teach as a group. Divide the team in half for drills. Each half practices on a separate diamond.	Leaving—Watch the ball; push off the back foot; listen to the base coach. Tagging up—Watch the ball; leave and return; listen to the base coach.
Teach 15 min (45 min)	Force-outs/Tag-outs Force-out-Tag-out Drill	Teach as a group. Divide the team in half for drill. Each half practices on separate diamonds.	Force-outs—Move to the base; touch the base; catch the ball. Tag-outs—Stand behind the base; catch the ball; place the glove in front of the runner.
Teach 10 min (55 min)	Bunt Coverage Bunt Reaction Drill	Teach as a group. Divide the team in half for the drills.	Charge the ball; call for the ball; back up players and move to the bases.
Teach 15 min (70 min)	Playing Strategy Playing Strategy Drill	Teach as a group. Use the discussion in *Softball Coaches Guide*.	Involve players in the discussion. Stress the priority of the rules.
Practice 15 min (85 min)	Pitching/Catching Throwing and catching pitches	Pair up for the drills. Pitch from regulation distance.	Pitching—Pitch accurately; stride toward the target; follow-through. Catching—Watch the ball; trap the ball.
Cool-down/ Evaluation 5 min (90 min)	Easy throwing, jogging, stretching	Choose 2 players to lead the cool-down. Cool down as a group.	Review the practice. Mention time and place for next practice. Wear proper clothing for sliding practice.

Practice Plan 5

Age: 13 and up
Total time: 90 minutes

Instructional Goals
Practice fielding skills, positional skills, pitching and catching. Teach how to place hits, slide, and make double plays.

Equipment
Balls, bats, helmets, 2 sets of catching equipment, 2 sets of bases, sliding equipment
For the coach: Player roster, practice plans, first-aid kit

Drills
Fielding—Outfield Ground Ball-Fly Ball Drill; Infield-Outfield Drill
Positional Skills—Individual Position Drill; Infield and Outfield Drill
Pitching/Catching—Hit the Mitt Drill
Batting—Batting/Fielding Drill
Baserunning—Sliding practice
Team Defense—Receiving Tosses Drill; Double Play Practice Drill

Component/Time	Activity/Drills	Organization	Coaching Points
Warm-up 5 min	Easy stretching, jogging, throwing	Choose 2 players to lead the warm-up.	Discuss today's practice.
Practice 15 min (20 min)	Fielding Outfield Ground Ball-Fly Ball Drill Infield and Outfield Drill (infield only)	Divide the infielders, outfielders, pitchers, and catchers. Fielders practice fielding; pitchers and catchers practice pitching.	Outfield—Move to the ball; watch the ball, and keep the ball in front. Infield—Move to the ball; trap the ball; throw accurately.
Practice 15 min (20 min)	Pitching/Catching Hit the Mitt Drill	Separate the pitchers/catchers from the team. Practice on a separate field while the fielders practice together.	Pitching—Proper arm swing, stride, wrist snap, and follow-through. Catching—Present a good target; watch and trap the ball.
Teach 15 min (35 min)	Batting-Placing Hits Batting/Fielding Drill	Teach as a group. Divide team in half for drill. Each half practices on a separate field.	Use the contact angle to direct hits. Time the pitch; step open or closed.
Teach 20 min (55 min)	Double Plays Receiving Tosses Drill Double Play Practice Drill	Teach as a group. Divide team in half for practice. Have both infielders and outfielders practice double plays.	Toss the ball easily. Touch and step away from the base. Throw accurately to first base.
Practice 15 min (70 min)	Positional Play Individual Position Drill Infield and Outfield Drill	Divide team in half. Each coach conducts one drill on separate fields. Rotate players after 7 min.	Be aware of the coverage areas and responsibilities. Encourage hustle and communication.
Teach 15 min (85 min)	Sliding Sliding practice	Set up the field for sliding (wet plastic, grass, or loose dirt). Demonstrate and teach as a group.	Bend the back leg; sit down on the thigh and hip; hold the hands up.
Cool-down/ Evaluation 5 min (90 min)	Easy throwing, jogging, stretching	Cool-down if the players are not wet. If they are wet, review the practice and dismiss.	Review the practice. Point out good skills and those which need work. Practice game for next session.

Practice Plan 6

Age: 13 and up
Total time: 90 minutes

Instructional Goals
Practice the fundamental skills in a practice game. Review and practice fielding, batting, baserunning, pitching, and catching to prepare for the game. Teach catchers how to shift and block pitches.

Equipment
Balls, bats, 2 sets of catching equipment, 2 sets of bases, helmets
For the coach: Player roster, practice plans, first-aid kit

Drills
Fielding—Infield and Outfield Drill
Batting—Bunt Drill; Batting practice
Baserunning—Running the Bases Drill
Pitching/Catching—Shift Drill; Hit the Mitt Drill
Practice Game—Practice Game Drill

Component/Time	Activity/Drills	Organization	Coaching Points
Warm-up 5 min	Easy throwing, jogging, stretching	Choose 2 players to lead the warm-up.	Warm up easily. Discuss today's practice.
Practice 15 min (20 min)	Fielding Infield and Outfield Drill	Divide the team in half. Separate the pitchers and catchers. Pitchers and catchers practice together.	Move to the ball; watch the ball. Communicate with other fielders. Throw accurately.
Teach/Practice 15 min (35 min)	Pitching/Catching Shift Drill Hit the Mitt Drill	Separate the pitchers and catchers. Teach catchers to shift and block pitches. Practice pitching and catching.	Catching—Shift with the hips; block pitches with the mitt. Pitching—Stress accuracy.
Practice 15 min (35 min)	Batting Bunt Drill Batting practice	Divide the team in half. Practice on separate diamonds.	Bunt—Square to the ball; try to catch the ball; place the bunt. Hitting—Swing level; step into the pitch; watch the ball.
Practice 10 min (45 min)	Baserunning Running the Bases Drill	Divide the team in half. Practice on separate diamonds.	Step toward first base. Do not leap upon the bases. Swing wide, turn in, and touch the corner.
Practice 40 min (85 min)	Practice Practice Game Drill	Divide the team in half.	Stress proper mechanics, team communication, and backing up. Let them have fun.
Cool-down/ Evaluation 5 min (90 min)	Easy throwing, jogging, stretching	Choose 2 players to lead the cool-down.	Review the practice. Mention time and place of next practice.

Practice Plan 7

Age: 13 and up
Total time: 75 minutes

Instructional Goals
Practice fielding, batting, team defense, pitching, and catching. Teach the windmill-pitching style.

Equipment
Balls, bats, helmets, 2 sets of catching equipment, 2 sets of bases
For the coach: Player roster, practice plans, first-aid kit

Drills
Fielding—Infield and Outfield Drill; Outfield Ground Ball-Fly Ball Drill
Batting—Batting practice
Team Defense—Game Situation Drill; Backing-up Drill
Pitching/Catching—Shift Drill; Throwing and catching pitches

Component/Time	Activity/Drills	Organization	Coaching Points
Warm-up 5 min	Easy stretching, jogging, throwing	Choose 2 players to lead the warm-up.	Discuss today's practice. Keep the warm-up easy.
Practice 15 min (20 min)	Fielding Infield and Outfield Drill (infielders) Outfield Ground Ball-Fly Ball Drill	Divide the infielders, outfielders, pitchers, and catchers. Infielders practice together. Outfielders practice together. Pitchers and catchers practice pitching.	Use the glove correctly. Trap the ball; keep the ball in front.
Teach/Practice 15 min (20 min)	Pitching/Catching Shift Drill Hit the Mitt Drill	Teach the windmill style while catchers practice shifting. Practice pitching and catching.	Pitching—Swing the arm up and around without pausing; step toward the target; follow-through.
Practice 30 min (50 min)	Batting Bunt Drill Batting practice	Divide the team in half. Practice drills separately, and switch players after 15 min.	Square to bunt and place the ball. Swing level and watch the ball.
Practice 20 min (70 min)	Team Defense Game Situation Drill Backing-up Drill	Divide the team in half. Practice each drill on a separate diamond. Switch after 10 min.	Stress communication, hustle, and knowing where to throw. Back up about 10 ft behind the fielder.
Cool-down/ Evaluation 5 min (75 min)	Easy throwing, jogging, stretching	Choose two players to lead the cool-down.	Review the practice; compliment their effort and skills. Next session is a practice game.

Practice Plan 8

Age: 13 and up
Total time: 90 minutes

Instructional Goals
Practice fielding, baserunning, team defense, pitching and catching in preparation for a practice game.

Equipment
Balls, bats, helmets, 2 sets of bases, 2 sets of catching equipment
For the coach: Player roster, practice plans, first-aid kit

Drills
Fielding—Fielding Ground Balls Drill; Judging Fly Balls Drill
Baserunning—Running the Bases Drill
Team Defense—Cut-off and Relay Drill; Backing-up Drill
Pitching/Catching—Hit the Mitt Drill
Practice Game—Practice Game Drill

Component/Time	Activity/Drills	Organization	Coaching Points
Warm-up 5 min	Easy stretching, jogging, throwing	Choose 2 players to lead the warm-up.	Discuss today's practice.
Practice 20 min (25 min)	Fielding Fielding Ground Balls Drill Judging Fly Balls Drill	Divide the team in half. Each half practices on a separate field. Switch players after 10 min. Separate pitchers and catchers.	Watch the ball and move to the ball; keep the ball in front; trap the ball.
	Pitching/Catching	Separate pitchers and catchers from other fielders. Pitch and catch in a separate area.	Pitching—Work on both styles; pitch accurately. Catching—Keep the ball in front; block poor pitches.
Practice 10 min (35 min)	Baserunning Running the Bases Drill	Divide the team in half and practice on separate diamonds.	Run fast, but under control. Do not leave the base early.
Practice 10 min (45 min)	Team Defense Cut-off and Relay Drill Backing-up Drill	Divide the team into groups of 3 to 5 players. Switch drills after 5 min.	Throw accurately; use the skip and throw. Back up 10 ft behind the fielder. Watch the ball.
Practice 40 min (85 min)	Practice Game Practice Game Drill	Divide the team in half.	Encourage and compliment hustle and effort. Let them have fun. Correct skills constructively.
Cool-down/ Evaluation 5 min (90 min)	Easy throwing, jogging, stretching	Choose 2 players to lead the cool-down.	Review the practice. Mention time and place of first game.

Chapter 13: Playing Games and Evaluating Performances

Game time should be the most enjoyable and fun part of the season—for coaches and for players. If you and your players have worked hard during practices, you will be ready to have fun playing well and competing with another team. Winning is important, but one team will win and one team will lose. We urge you to keep winning in perspective by stressing the fun of playing well and competing, rather than the outcome of the game.

Getting ready for each game does require a little extra work by the coach. This chapter covers (a) warming up for games, (b) keeping game score, (c) establishing a batting order, and (d) what to do after each game.

Warming Up for Games

A proper warm-up is just as important for actual game preparation as it is for practice preparation. In fact, the pregame warm-up should be similar to the warm-up during practices. Be sure your players exercise the arms, legs, stomach, and back, beginning with easy exercises and progressing to more strenuous ones.

The pregame warm-up should include practicing skills specific to the position your players are assigned. Tell your players which positions they will play at the practice before each game

or well before the game begins. Also, allow enough time for players who do not start the game to warm-up prior to entering the game later. Traditionally, pitchers are the only players who warm up after the game begins. However, in order to play well and to prevent injuries, every player should warm up properly before entering the game.

How can you make sure your players are warmed up and ready to play when you need them? A good method is to determine (a) which positions each will play, (b) how many innings he or she will play in that position, (c) when substitutes will enter the game, and (d) which positions the substitutes will play. By planning your game strategy well ahead of time, each player will be able to play several innings, know when he or she will enter the game, and be motivated to warm up properly.

The Batting Order

In addition to planning players' positions, it is a good idea to plan the batting order. If you are not familiar with how to determine the batting order, some guidelines follow. These guidelines consider the abilities of each batter and how these abilities influence game playing strategy.

- Assign the *leadoff* batting position to a player who has a good eye for the strike zone, is not afraid to swing, but is also willing to wait for a walk.
- The *second* batter should be a good bunter, or be able to contact the ball well, and a good baserunner.
- The *third* batter will often be in position to move other players around the bases or will need to get on with 2 outs. This means the third batter should be able to place the ball and run the bases well.
- The *fourth* batter is often called the *clean-up* batter because there may be two or three runners on base, and the bases will need to be cleared or cleaned up. Consequently, the fourth batter should be able to hit the ball hard.
- The *fifth* batter can come to bat with 1 or 2 outs and two or more runners on base, and should also be a hard hitter.
- The *sixth* batter can be considered a second leadoff batter and may often be the first batter in a new inning.
- Because the *seventh* batter follows the second leadoff batter, he or she should have abilities similar to the second batter.
- The *eighth* batter should have abilities similar to the third batter.
- The *ninth* batter is traditionally the poorest batter. Because many older players specialize in their positions, the pitcher is often scheduled as the last batter. In youth softball, the pitcher is usually a good athlete who can hit well and should be placed wherever he or she will most benefit the team.

In *slow-pitch* softball, where 10 players are in the batting order, the ninth batter will have characteristics similar to the eighth batter, and the tenth batter will be similar to the ninth as listed above.

Keeping Score

Keeping score will be relatively easy if you become familiar with a few abbreviations. Many scorebooks and rulebooks will help you by providing examples of how to score a game and of the abbreviations to use when keeping score. The following abbreviations are commonly used to designate player positions, walks, outs, baserunning, and scoring.

Numbers Designating Defensive Positions

Fast Pitch
1—Pitcher
2—Catcher
3—1st Baseman
4—2nd Baseman
5—3rd Baseman
6—Shortstop

7—Left Fielder
8—Center Fielder
9—Right Fielder
Slow Pitch
8—Left Center Fielder
9—Right Center Fielder
10—Right Fielder

Abbreviations Indicating Actions

W—Walk (BB—Base on balls)
K—Strike Out
Kc—Called Third Strike
E—Error
B—Balk
O—Out
FL—Foul Out
FO—Force-Out
H—Sacrifice
PB—Passed Ball
WP—Wild Pitch
HP—Hit by Pitch
DP—Double Play

TP—Triple Play
S—Stolen Base
OS—Out Stealing
FC—Fielder's Choice
SF—Sacrifice Fly
AB—Times at Bat
R—Runs
H—Hits
RBI—Runs Batted In
G—Ground Ball (for unassisted infield outs)
F—Fly Ball

What to Do After Each Game

As the season progresses, you will become more familiar with the abilities of your players and with your abilities as a coach. Each game will indicate the abilities of your players and your coaching effectiveness, giving you some direction for planning future practices. As a coach, you have three specific tasks after each game: (a) to evaluate playing ability, (b) to refine skills, and (c) to introduce new skills.

Evaluate Playing Ability

Take some time after each game to evaluate the playing abilities of your athletes and to determine which skills to work on. Decide if overall team play was above, below, or equal to the team's ability for this stage of the season. Determining what your players need to work on may or may not be obvious. Some errors are easily detected, while others are more difficult to discern.

Two coaching aids have been developed to help you evaluate playing ability and to monitor the progress of your team. These are the Individual Skills Checklist, and the Team Performance Checklist. The Individual Skills Checklist will help you monitor the skill development of each player practice by practice throughout the season and during games. The Team Performance Checklist will help you and your assistants evaluate the quality of team performance during games by identifying errors and evaluating possible causes for the errors. Outlines of these coaching aids can be found in Appendix C. Make copies of these checklists and use them during practices and games to chart the progress of your team.

Refining Skills

Refining skills can be a difficult and time-consuming process. Most often errors are not caused by complex, technical movement problems, but by simple, basic mistakes. Refer to the Softball Coaching Guide for an analysis of skill techniques and take steps to correct the skills as soon as possible. Improvements often come slowly, but as the pieces are put together, both you and your players will receive a great deal of personal satisfaction.

Introduce New Skills

As the season progresses and your players become more skilled and experienced, you may want to teach more advanced skills. For example, you can add bunting to the offense, double-play coverage and bunt coverage to the defense, or add other skills not covered in *Coaching Softball Effectively*. When you do teach more advanced skills, be sure not to go too far beyond the ability of your players. But do challenge them to perform new skills which they are physically and mentally capable of mastering.

Appendices

Appendix A: Softball Rules

The following rules have been condensed from the official rules adopted by the Amateur Softball Association (ASA) and by the Southern California Municipal Athletic Federation (SCMAF). These rules are not intended to replace an official rule book from the ASA, SCMAF, or any other organization, but are intended to provide you with basic softball rules in a simplified format. These rules follow the organizational format of the official ASA rules as closely as possible. Where discrepancies exist, such as exclusion of **Rule 1—Definitions** and **Rule 10—Umpires**, refer to the official ASA rule book, and consider it authoritative.

Rule 1. Definitions

Refer to the official ASA rule book.

Rule 2. The Playing Field

1. **The playing field** is the area within which the ball may be legally played or fielded.

2. **Ground or special rules** establishing the limits of the playing field may be agreed upon by leagues or opposing teams whenever backstops, fences, stands, vehicles, spectators, or other obstructions are within the prescribed area.

3. **The official diamond** shall have 60-ft baselines with a pitching distance of 46 ft, except as modified by the league.

4. **The layout of the diamond** is shown in the accompanying diagrams.

5. **The 3-foot line** is drawn parallel to and 3 ft from the baseline starting at a point halfway between home plate and first base, and extending to a point 3 ft beyond first base.

6. **The batter's box**, one on each side of home plate, shall measure 3 ft by 7 ft. The inside lines of the batter's box shall be 6 in. from home plate. The front line of the box shall be 4 ft in front of a line drawn through the center of home plate.

7. **The catcher's box** shall be 10 ft in length from the rear outside corners of the batter's boxes and shall be 8 ft 5 in. wide.

8. **The coach's box** is behind a line 15 ft long drawn outside the diamond.

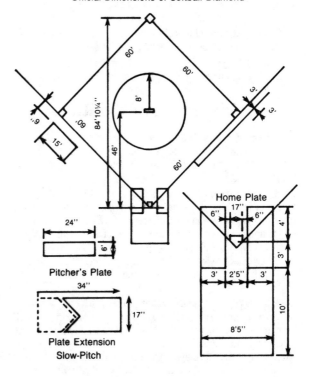

Official Dimensions of Softball Diamond

Pitcher's Plate

Plate Extension
Slow-Pitch

Home Plate

9. **The pitcher's plate**, made of either wood or rubber, shall measure 24 in. long and 6 in. wide.

10. **The pitcher's circle** shall measure an 8 ft radius from the center of the pitcher's plate.

11. **The home plate** shall be made of rubber or other suitable material. It shall be a five-sided figure 17 in. wide across the edge facing the pitcher.

12. **Fitness of diamond.** The question of fitness of a diamond for play shall be determined in advance by the director or supervisor of the area.

13. **Bases.** The bases, other than home plate shall be 15 in. square and shall be made of canvas or other suitable material. The bases shall be securely fastened in position.

Rule 3. Equipment

1. **The official bat.** The official bat shall be round, made of one-piece hardwood or one-piece seamless metal tubing that may only be open at barrel end with a rubber insert firmly secured. The bat

shall be not more than 34 in. long and not more than 2¼ in. in diameter at its largest part.

2. The official ball. Any ball which carries an ASA endorsement stamp is an approved ball.

3. Shoes. Shoes must be worn; bare feet will not be permitted. Metal cleats are not allowed. Use of molded rubber or multi-purpose shoes is recommended.

4. Gloves. A fielders glove may be worn by any players but mitts may be used only by the first baseman and catcher, and webbing of any glove between thumb and forefinger shall not exceed more than 4 in. in length.

5. Masks must be worn by catchers in fast-pitch. Optional for slow-pitch. Catchers must wear mask and chest protector in women's fast-pitch.

6. Warm-Up Bats. All players may loosen up with only one official softball bat or approved warm-up bat. No added equipment may be attached to a bat such as a donut or fan when loosening up.

7. Penalty for use of illegal equipment (with the exception of an illegal bat) shall be its removal from the game.

8. Penalty for use of illegal bat shall be: batter declared out, ball declared dead, and the illegal bat removed from the game.

Rule 4. Players and Substitutes

1. Nine players shall constitute a team. No team shall start a game with less than nine players and except for the pitcher and catcher, the team in the field may be stationed at any desirable point on fair ground.

2. A substitute may replace a player whose name appears in his or her team's batting order, but such relieved player shall not thereafter participate in the game except as a coach or manager. "A violation of this rule results in the use of an ineligible player. Upon discovery of the violation, the ineligible player must be immediately removed from the game and replaced with a legal substitute. If no legal substitute is available, then game shall be declared a forfeit."

3. A manager may have another player run for a base runner by and with the consent of the opposing captain or manager each time a runner is to be replaced, and when such permission is given, both the regular runner and the courtesy runner shall be eligible for further participation in the game. The player making the last official out in the inning shall be the designated runner.

4. In relieving a pitcher the new pitcher shall, unless incapacitated, continue to pitch until the batter then at bat or substitute has either been put out or has reached first, or the side has been retired.

5. On substitutions, whether for the batter, base runner or fielder, the manager making such changes must immediately notify the umpire who shall call time out and announce same to spectators, players, and scorekeepers. If through oversight such announcement is not made, the substitute shall not be called out.

6. Substitute players will be considered in the game on the following conditions: (a) If a pitcher, when he or she takes his or her place on the pitcher's plate. (b) If a batter, when he or she takes his or her place in the batter's box. (c) If a fielder, when he or she takes the place of the fielder substituted for and play is resumed. (d) If a runner, when the substitute replaces him or her on the base the runner is holding.

7. The offensive team: (a) Shall be allowed two coaches only, one near first base and one near third base, who shall remain within the coach's box at all times. (b) Shall not be allowed more than one (1) offensive conference each inning.

8. No manager, player, substitute, coach, trainer, or bat-keeper shall at any time, whether from the bench, the coach's box, on the playing field, or elsewhere: (a) Incite, or try to incite, by word or sign a demonstration by spectators. (b) Use language which will in any manner refer to or reflect upon opposing players, an umpire, or any spectator. (c) Call "Time" or employ any other word or phrase or commit any act while the ball is alive and in play for the obvious purpose of trying to make the pitcher commit an illegal pitch. (d) Take a position in the batter's line of vision, and with deliberate unsportsmanlike intent, act in a manner to distract the batter.

Rule 5. The Game

1. Softball is a game between two teams, under direction and control of a manager, played on an enclosed field in accordance with these rules, under jurisdiction of one or more umpires.

A fast-pitch team must field 9 players to start a game. Should an injury leave a team with only 8 eligible players, the game may continue.

A slow-pitch team shall consist of 10 players. However, a game may be played without forfeit with 9 rostered players.

2. The objective of each team is to win by scoring more runs than its opponent.

3. The winner of the game shall be that team which shall have scored in accordance with these rules, the greater number of runs at the conclusion of a regulation game.

4. The home team shall have first choice of innings.

5. A regulation game shall consist of seven innings, unless the team second at bat scores more runs in six innings than the team at bat scored in seven innings.

6. It is a regulation game when the team last at bat in the seventh inning scores the winning run before the third man is out.

7. It is a regulation game if it is called by the umpire on account of darkness, rain, fire, panic, or other cause which puts the patrons or players in peril provided four innings have been completed or if the home team has scored more runs in three or three and a fraction half-innings than the visiting team has scored in four complete half-innings.

8. When a game is called in any inning after the fourth, the score shall be what it was at the time the game was called.

9. If the game is tied at the end of seven innings, play shall be continued until one side has scored more runs than the other in an equal number of innings.

10. A regulation drawn game shall be declared by the umpire if the score is equal on the last even inning played, when the umpire terminates play in accordance with section 7 of this rule after each team has played four or more complete innings.

11. Forfeited games. A forfeited game shall be declared by the umpire in favor of the team not at fault in the following cases: (a) If a team fails to appear upon the field, or being upon the field, refuses to begin a game for which it is scheduled or assigned at the time scheduled or within the time set for forfeitures by the organization in which the team is playing. (b) If, after the game has begun, one side refuses to continue to play, unless the game has been suspended or terminated by the umpire. (c) If, after play has been suspended by the umpire, one side fails to resume playing within 2 minutes after the umpire has called "Play ball." (d) If a team employs tactics designed to delay or to hasten the game. (e) If, after warning by the umpire, any one of the rules of the game is willfully violated. (f) If the order for the removal of a player is not obeyed within 1 minute. (g) If, because of the removal of a player or players from the game by the umpire, or for any cause, there are less than 9 players on either team, except for fast-pitch. (h) Game officials have the authority to forfeit a game when they feel the situation is such that physical harm may come to themselves, players, or spectators.

12. The score of a forfeited game shall be 7–0 in favor of the offended team.

Rule 6. Pitching Regulations

Penalty for illegal pitches. Any infractions of sections 1-12 shall be considered as an illegal pitch. The ball is dead. A ball is called in favor of the batter. Base runners are entitled to advance one base without liability to be put out. The ball shall remain dead until put in play at the pitcher's plate.

1. Preliminary to pitching, the pitcher shall make a presentation by coming to a full and complete stop facing the batter with shoulders in line with first and third base, with the ball held with both hands in front of his or her body (between the knees and the face) and with both feet in contact with the pitcher's rubber. (a) If a signal is taken, it must be taken from the pitcher's plate. (b) He or she shall hold the ball for not less than 1 second and not more than 10 seconds before releasing the ball. (c) The pitcher shall not be considered in pitching position unless the catcher is in position to receive the pitch. (d) The pitcher may not take the pitching position on or near the pitcher's plate without having the ball in his or her possession.

2. The pitch starts when one hand is taken off the ball or the pitcher makes any motion that is part of his or her windup following the presentation of the ball. In the act of delivering the ball, the pitcher shall not take more than one step, which must be forward, toward the batter and simultaneous with the delivery of the ball to the batter.

3. A legal delivery shall be a ball that is delivered to the batter with an underhand motion. (a) The release of the ball and the follow-through of the hand and wrist must be forward past the straight line of the body. (b) The hand shall be below the hip and the wrist not farther from the body than the elbow. (c) The pitch is completed with a step forward toward the batter. (d) The catcher must be within the outside lines of the catcher's box when the pitch is released.

4. The pitcher may use any windup he or she desires provided: (a) He or she does not make any motion to pitch without immediately delivering the ball to the batter. (b) He or she does not use a rocker action in which, after having the ball in both hands in pitching position, he or she removes one hand from the ball, takes a backward and forward swing, and returns the ball to both hands in front of the body. (c) He or she does not use a windup in which there is a stop or reversal of the forward motion. (d) He or she does not make more than one revolution of the arm in the windmill pitch. (e) He or she does not continue to wind up after the forward step which is simultaneous with the release of the ball.

5. The pitcher shall not drop the ball while in pitching position.

6. The pitcher shall not at any time during the game be allowed to use tape or other substance upon the ball, the pitching hand, or fingers. Under the supervision and control of the umpire, powdered rosin may be used to dry the hands.

7. In making a legal delivery, the pitcher may make contact with his or her clothing or body with his or her hand or the ball.

8. At the beginning of each inning or when a pitcher relieves another, no more than 1 minute may be used to deliver no more than five balls to the catcher or other teammate. Play shall be suspended during this time.

9. There shall be only one charged conference between the manager or other team representative from the dugout with each and every pitcher in an inning. The second charged conference shall result in the removal of the pitcher from the pitching position for the remainder of the game.

10. The pitcher shall not throw to a base while his or her foot is in contact with the pitcher's plate after he or she has taken the pitching position.

11. If the ball slips from the pitcher's hand during his or her windup or during the backswing, the ball will be in play and the runners may advance at their own risk.

12. No pitch shall be declared when: (a) The pitcher pitches during suspension of play. (b) The pitcher attempts a quick return of the ball before the batter has taken position or is off balance as a result of a previous pitch. (c) The runner is called out for leaving the base too soon.

13. Pitching rules (12" and 16" slow-pitch).
Legal Delivery—The pitcher shall conform to all fast-pitch pitching regulations with the following exceptions: (a) The pitcher shall deliver the ball to the batter at a moderate speed. (b) The ball must arc higher than the batter's head. (c) For 12" and 16" slow-pitch, the ball must not exceed a height of more than 12 ft above the ground. (d) The pitcher must present the ball in one or both hands with one foot or both feet in contact with the pitcher's rubber. (e) Pitcher must release the ball with one or both feet on the rubber; as the ball is released, the pitcher may take one step in any direction.
Legal deliveries are solely the judgment of the umpire and not protestable.
Illegal Delivery— (a) If any of the fast-pitch pitching regulations listed in Rule 4, sections 1 thru 12, are violated or any of the above speed, arc, or height rules are violated, the pitch shall be called a ball. Base runners do not advance. (b) If the batter attempts to hit an illegal delivery, the pitched ball will be considered as legal. (c) A pitched ball (swung at or not) that touches the ground before crossing or touching home plate will be declared dead. If any ball touches the ground and is then hit by the batter, the pitch is ruled a strike and the ball is declared dead.

Rule 7. Batting

1. The batter shall take position in the batter's box promptly when it is his or her time at bat: (a) The batter shall not have either one or both feet touching the ground entirely outside the lines of the batter's box when the ball is hit. (b) If the batter's bat hits the ball fair or foul while any portion of his or her body is touching home plate, he or she shall be declared out. (c) The batter shall not step to the other side of the plate while the pitcher is in position ready to pitch. Penalty: Batter declared out. (d) The batter must take position after the umpire declares "Play."

2. Each player of the side at bat shall become a batter in the order in which his or her name appears on the scoresheet. (a) The batting order of each team must be on the scoresheet and must be delivered before the game by the manager or captain to the plate umpire, who shall submit it for inspection by the manager or captain of the opposing team. (b) The batting order delivered to the umpire must be followed throughout the game unless a player is substituted for another, in which case the substitute must take the place of the removed player in the batting order. All defensive players must bat. (c) The first batter in each inning shall be the batter whose name follows that of the last player who completed his or her turn at bat in the preceding inning.

3. Batting out of order is an appeal play: (a) If the error is discovered while the incorrect batter is at bat, the correct batter may take his or her place and assume any balls and strikes; any runs scored or bases run while the incorrect batter was at bat shall be legal. (b) If the error is discovered after the incorrect batter has completed his or her turn at bat and before there has been a pitch to another batter, the player who should have batted is out. (c) If the error is discovered after the first pitch to the next batter, the time at bat of the incorrect batter is legal, all runs scored and bases run are legal, and the next batter in order shall be the one whose name follows that of the incorrect batter. (d) When the third out in an inning is made before the batter has completed his or her turn at bat, he or she shall be the first batter in the next inning.

4. The batter shall not hinder the catcher from fielding or throwing the ball by stepping out of the batter's box or intentionally hinder the catcher while standing within the batter's box.

5. Members of the team at bat shall not interfere with a player attempting to field a foul fly ball.

6. The batter shall not intentionally strike or bunt the ball a second time, strike it with a thrown bat, or deflect its course in any way while running to first base.

7. A strike is called by the umpire: (a) For each legally-pitched ball entering the strike zone before touching the ground at which the batter does not swing. (b) For each legally-pitched ball struck at and missed by the batter. (c) For each foul hit not caught on the fly unless the batsman has two strikes. (d) For each pitched ball at which the batsman strikes but misses and which touches any part of his or her person. (e) For each foul tip held by the catcher.

8. A ball is called by the umpire: (a) For each pitched ball which does not enter the strike zone or touches the ground before reaching home plate and which is not struck at by the batter. (b) For each illegally pitched ball (see illegal pitches).
The catcher must return the ball directly to the pitcher; unless a strikeout or put out is made by the catcher, a ball will be called in favor of the batter for each player other than the pitcher who handles the ball. A batter does not get his or her base when hit by a pitched ball (slow-pitch).

9. The batter is out under the following circumstances: (a) After three strikes. (b) When fair or foul fly ball (other than a foul tip) is legally caught by a fielder. (c) When after having two strikes, the batter hits a second foul ball (four-strike rule in slow-pitch). (d) When the batter bunts foul on a third strike.

10. The batter becomes a runner and is entitled to first base without liability to be put out (provided he or she advances to and touches first base) when: (a) ''Four balls'' have been called by the umpire. (b) He or she is touched by a pitched ball which he or she is not attempting to hit. (c) The catcher or any fielder interferes with him or her. If a play follows the interference, the manager of the offense may advise the plate umpire that he or she elects to decline the interference penalty and accept the play. (d) A fair ball touches an umpire or a runner on fair territory before touching a fielder. (e) The umpire may award an intentional walk to the batter upon the request of the manager (slow-pitch).

11. The batter becomes a base runner when: (a) He or she hits a fair ball. (b) A fair ball strikes the person or clothing of an umpire on fair ground. (c) The catcher interferes with or prevents the batter from striking at a pitched ball. (d) A pitched ball not struck at touches any part of the batter's person or clothing while he or she is in the batter's box, provided he or she makes an honest attempt to avoid being hit. (e) The third strike called by the umpire is not caught, providing: (1) first base is unoccupied, or (2) first base is occupied with two outs (fast-pitch only).

Rule 8. Baserunning

1. The base runner must touch bases in legal order: first, second, third, and home plate. When a base runner must return while the ball is in play, he or she must touch the bases in reverse order.

2. Base runners are entitled to advance without liability to be put out under the following conditions: (a) when forced to vacate a base because the batter was awarded a base on balls (one base); (b) when a fielder or umpire obstructs the base runner from making a base unless the fielder is trying to field a batted ball or has the ball ready to touch the base runner.

3. A player forfeits exemption from liability to be put out: (a) If while the ball is in play, he or she fails to touch the base to which he or she was entitled before attempting to make the next base. If the runner put out is batter/base runner at first base, or any other base runner forced to advance because the batter became a base runner, this out is a force-out. (b) If after overrunning first base, the batter/base runner attempts to continue to second base. (c) If after dislodging the base, the batter/base runner tries to continue to the next base.

4. The base runners advance is limited: (a) When a fair-batted fly ball goes over the fence or into the stand, it shall entitle the batter to a home run unless it passes out of the grounds or into a stand at a distance less than 250 ft from the home base, in which case the batter shall be entitled to two bases only. The point at which the fence or stand is less than 250 ft from the home base shall be plainly indicated for the umpire's guidance. (b) When any bounding fair ball is deflected by the fielder into dead ball territory, or over or under a fence on fair or foul territory in which case the batter and all runners shall be entitled to advance two bases beyond the base they occupied at the time of the pitch. Note: If in the umpire's judgment, a fielder intentionally throws, kicks, or carries ball into dead ball territory, the umpire may award as many bases he or she feels the runner(s) would have reached.

5. The base runner must return to his or her base under the following circumstances: (a) When a foul ball is illegally caught and is so declared by the umpire. (b) When an illegally-batted ball is so declared by the umpire. (c) When a batter or base runner is called out for interference. (d) When there is interference by the plate umpire or his or her clothing with the catcher's attempt to throw.

6. Batter/base runners are out under the following circumstances: (a) When after a fair ball is hit, he or she is legally touched with the ball before he or she touches first base. (b) When after a fair ball, the ball is held by a fielder touching first base with any part of his or her person before the batter/base runner touches first base. (c) When after a fly ball, the ball is caught by a fielder before it touches the ground or any object other than a fielder. (d) When he or she runs outside the 3-foot line and, in the opinion of the umpire, interferes with the fielder taking the throw at first base.

7. The base runner is out under the following circumstances: (a) When in running to any base, he or she runs more than 3 ft from a direct line between a base and the next one in regular or reverse order to avoid being touched by the ball in the hand of a fielder. (b) When, while the ball is in play, he or she is legally touched with the ball in the hand of a fielder while not in contact with a base. (c) When, on a force-out, a fielder holds the ball on the base to which the base runner is forced to advance before the runner reaches that base. (d) When the umpire calls the base runner out for failure to return to touch the base when play is resumed after a suspension of play. (e) When a base runner passes a preceding base runner before that runner has been put out. (f) When a base runner leaves his or her base to advance to another base before a fly ball has been touched, providing the ball is returned to a fielder and legally held on that base or legally touches the base runner before the runner can return. (g) When the base runner fails to touch the intervening base or bases in regular or reverse order and the ball is in play and legally held on that base, or the base runner is legally touched while off base. (h) When the base runner is legally touched while off base. (i) When a base runner interferes or obstructs a fielder attempting to field a batted ball or intentionally interferes with a thrown ball. (j) When the base runner is struck by a fair ball in fair territory before the ball has touched or passed an infielder.

8. Base runners are not out under the following circumstances: (a) When a base runner runs behind the fielder and outside the baselines in order to avoid interfering with a fielder attempting to field the ball in the base path. (b) When a base runner does not run in a direct line to the base providing the fielder in the direct lines does not have the ball in his or her possession. (c) When more than one fielder attempts to field a batted ball and the base runner comes in contact with the one who, in the umpire's judgment, was not entitled to field the ball. (d) When a base runner is hit with a fair ball that has passed through an infielder and, in the umpire's judgment, no other fielder had a chance to play the ball. (e) When a base runner is touched with the ball not securely held by a fielder. (f) When the defensive team does not request the umpire's decision on an appeal play until after the next pitch. (g) When the base runner overturns first base after touching it and returns directly to the base.

Rule 9. Dead Ball—Ball in Play

1. The ball is dead and not in play under the following circumstances: (a) When a pitched ball touches any part of the batter's person or clothing while the batter is standing in his or her position, whether the ball is struck at or not. (b) When a ball is batted illegally. (c) When "no pitch" is declared. (d) When a batter steps from one box to another when the pitcher is ready to pitch. (e) When a foul ball is not legally caught. (f) When a base runner is called out for leaving the base too soon. (g) When the offensive team causes an interference. (h) When a wild pitch or passed ball goes under, over or through a backstop, or lodges in the umpire's mask or paraphernalia. (i) When an overthrow touches any obstruction of person other than spectator protection fence or players in the game. (j) When a play is completed and runners are stopped and attempting no further advance, the umpire shall declare "Time-Out." (k) When a ball is pitched illegally. (l) When the catcher interferes with the batter. (m) When a legally caught fly ball in playable territory is carried by the fielder unintentionally into dead ball territory, the ball is dead, the batter is out, and all runners advance one base beyond the base they occupied at the time of the pitch. If in the judgment of the umpire, the fielder intentionally carries a legally caught fly ball into dead ball territory, the ball is dead, the batter is out, and all runners are awarded two bases beyond the base they occupied at the time of the pitch. (n) When the umpire calls "Time." (o) The umpire may award an intentional walk to the batter upon the request of the manager (slow-pitch). (p) When a batter receives an intentional walk, the ball is dead—base runners may advance only if forced.

2. The ball is alive and in play: (a) When after a fly ball, either fair, foul, or foul tip has been legally caught. (b) When after four balls have been called, provided, however, that the batter cannot be put out before reaching first base. (c) When after interference by a fielder with a base runner, provided that the runner interfered with cannot be put out before he or she reaches the base to which he or she is entitled. (d) When the infield fly rule is enforced. (e) When a thrown or pitched ball goes into foul territory and is not obstructed. (f) When a thrown or pitched ball strikes an umpire. (g) When a thrown ball goes past a fielder and remains in live territory. (h) When a fair ball strikes an umpire or base runner on fair ground after passing or touching fielder. (i) When a fair ball strikes an umpire on foul ground. (j) When the base runners have reached the bases to which they are entitled and the fielder illegally fields a batted or thrown ball. (k) When a base runner is called out for passing a preceding runner. (l) When the ball is not dead. (m) When after base runners have reached the bases to which they are entitled.

3. Appeals: (a) When the ball is alive, any fielder may appeal any runner once: The ball is alive and all runners may advance with liability of being put out. (b) To make appeals after a dead ball or "Time Out" is called, the following procedures must be used: *Pitcher must be in position, have possession of the ball, and the umpire signals "Play Ball" (the ball is alive and in play). *The pitcher must step clearly back from the pitching plate before throwing or carrying the ball to the base the appeal is to be made. If the pitcher makes an appeal and is in contact with the pitching plate at the time of the throw, an illegal pitch is called. (A ball on the batter, all base runners advance one base, and the ball is dead). *Note: Runners do not advance in slow-pitch. (c) The defensive team can have only one attempted appeal per runner but may appeal more than one runner per play. (d) If, during any appeal, the ball is thrown or bounds into dead ball territory, the ball is dead, all runners advance two bases without liability of being put out, and the defense may not appeal again during that play. (e) Any appeal under this rule must be made before the next pitch or any play or attempted play. If the violation occurs during a play which ends a half inning, the appeal must be made before the defensive team leaves the field. (f) An appeal is not to be interpreted as a play or an attempted play. (g) Runners may advance at their own risk during an appeal. (h) No runner is out if he or she steps off base during an appeal.

Rule 10. Umpires

Refer to the official ASA rule book.

Rule 11. Protests

1. The notification of intent to protest must be made immediately before the next pitch. (a) The captain or manager of the protesting team should immediately notify the umpires and the opponent that the game is being continued under protest. (b) All interested parties shall take notice of the conditions surrounding the making of a decision that will aid in the correct determination of the issue.

2. Protests that shall be received and considered are: (a) Misinterpretation of a playing rule. (b) Failure of an umpire to apply the correct rule to a given situation. (c) Failure to impose the correct penalty for a given violation.

3. Protests may involve both a matter of judgment and the interpretations of a rule. An example of a situation of this type follows: With one out and the runners on second and third base, the batter flied out, the runner on third tagged up after the catch, the player on second did not. The runner on third crossed the plate before the ball was played at second base for the third out. The umpire did not allow the run to score. The question as to whether the runners left their bases before the catch and whether the play at second base was made before the player to third crossed the plate are solely matters of judgment and not protestable. The failure of the umpire to allow the run to score was a misinterpretation of a playing rule and was a proper subject for protest.

4. Protests shall not be received or considered if they are based solely on a decision involving the accuracy of judgment on the part of the umpire.

5. The protest must be filed within a reasonable length of time: (a) In the absence of a league or tournament rule fixing the time limit for filing a protest, a protest should be considered if filed within a reasonable time, depending upon the nature of the case and the difficulty of obtaining the information on which to base the protest. (b) Within 48 hours after the scheduled time of the contest is generally considered a reasonable length of time.

6. A formal protest should contain the following information: (a) The date, time, and place of game. (b) The names of the umpires and the scorer. (b) The names of the umpires and the scorer. (c) The rule and section of the official rules or local rules under which the protest is made. (d) The decision and conditions surrounding the making of the decision. (e) All essential facts involved in the matter protested.

7. The decision made on a protested game may result in one of the following: (a) The protest is found invalid and the game score stands as played. (b) When a protest is allowed for misinterpretation of a playing rule, the game is replayed from the point at which the incorrect decision was made with decision corrected. (c) When a protest for ineligibility is allowed, the offended team shall be credited with a victory. (Forfeit score 7-0).

Rule 12. Scoring of Runs

1. One run shall be scored every time a base runner, after having legally touched the first three bases, shall legally touch the home base before three players are out; provided, however, that if the runner reaches home on or during a play in which the third player is forced out or is put out before reaching first base, a run shall not count; also, if the third out is made by a preceding runner failing to touch a base, a run shall not count.

2. When a pitch is started, a runner on base cannot score on any pitched ball that passes the batter, except when the bases are full and the runner is forced to advance by reason of the batter becoming a base runner by reason of a base on balls or catcher's interference (slow-pitch only).

3. A runner, when the pitch is started, may score: (a) On a fair hit ball. (b) On a foul fly ball that is legally caught. (c) On a play on any runner (fast-pitch only). (d) If the ball is thrown to any other player except the pitcher (fast-pitch only). (e) On a passed ball, wild pitch, or return from catcher (fast-pitch). (f) On an illegal pitch (fast-pitch only). (g) On catcher's interference, if forced.

Rule 13. Players Code of Conduct

1. No player shall at any time lay a hand upon, push, shove, strike, or threaten to strike an official.

2. No player shall refuse to abide by officials' decision.

3. No player shall be guilty of objectionable demonstrations by throwing of gloves, bats, balls, or any other forceful action.

4. No player shall be guilty of heaping personal, verbal abuse upon any official for any real or imaginary wrong decision or judgment.

5. No player shall discuss with an official in any manner the decision reached by such official except the manager or captain.

6. No player shall be guilty of using unnecessarily rough tactics in the play of the game against the body and person of any opposing player.

7. No player shall be guilty of physical attack as an aggressor, upon any player, official, or spectator.

8. No player shall be guilty of abusive verbal attack upon any player, official, or spectator.

9. No player shall use profane, obscene, or vulgar language in any manner or at any time.

10. No player shall appear on the field of play at any time in an intoxicated condition.

11. No player shall be guilty of gambling upon any play or the outcome of the game with any spectator, player, or opponent.

12. No player shall smoke while going on or coming off the field of play or while on the field of play.

13. No player shall be guilty of publicly discussing with players any play, decision, or personal opinion of other players in a derogatory or abusive manner during the game.

14. No player shall permit anyone who is not a playing member of the team to remain in the dugout or on the player's bench during the game.

15. No player shall be guilty of intentionally throwing his or her bat.

Appendix B: Instructional Schedule and Practice Plan Outlines

4-Week Instructional Schedule for Youth Softball

Goal: To help players learn and practice individual and team skills needed to play a regulation game after 4 weeks.

T(10): Teach skill for first time in 10 min.
P(10): Practice or drill the skill for 10 min.

*: These skill components are practiced during the drills for this playing category.

Skills	Week 1		Week 2		Week 3		Week 4		Time in
	Day 1	Day 2	Day 3	Day 4	Day 5	Day 6	Day 7	Day 8	Minutes
Throwing/Catching									
Fielding									
Batting									
Baserunning									
Positional Skills									
Team Defense									
Game Play									
Pitching									
Catching									

Practice Plan #____

Total time: 80 minutes

Instructional Goals

Drills

Equipment

Component/Time	Activity/Drills	Organization	Coaching Points

Practice Plan #____

Appendix C:
Individual Skills
Checklist and
Team Performance
Checklist Outlines

Individual Skills Checklist

Practice (game) _____

Evaluate skills as: Good, O.K., Needs work

Name	Hitting/ Bunting	Running Bases	Throwing/ Catching	Position/ Fielding	Team-Play	Comments/ Suggestions

Team Performance Checklist

Game _____

Evaluate skills as: Good, O.K., Needs work

Team Play	Good	O.K.	Needs Work	Additional Comments
Hustle				
Back-up play				
Relay and cut-off				
Baserunning				
Communication				
Following instructions				
Pitching				
Batting				
Coaching help				
Base coaching				
Attitude				
Instructions and comments				

Appendix D:
Coaching Softball
Effectively
Evaluation

Tell Us What You Think

It is our commitment at ACEP to provide coaches with the most complete, accurate, and useful information available. Our authors, consultants, and editors are continuously searching for new ideas and are constantly seeking to improve our materials. Now that you have read and studied this book, it is your turn to tell us what you liked and did not like about it. Please take a few minutes to complete the following survey and send it to: ACEP, Box 5076, Champaign, IL 61820.

Book Evaluation for
Coaching Softball Effectively

Instructions: For each statement, mark the spaces in the left-hand column which corresponds to what you think of this book. We are interested in your opinions so feel free to mark more than one response to each statement.

1. The organization of this book
____ (a) presents material in an easy to understand progression
____ (b) is helpful
____ (c) is confusing

2. The material presented in this book is
____ (a) easy to read and understand
____ (b) difficult to read and understand
____ (d) too simple
____ (e) too complex

3. Figures and illustrations are
____ (a) helpful
____ (b) distracting
____ (c) technically correct
____ (d) technically incorrect
____ (e) confusing

4. Coaching points and teaching progressions
____ (a) highlight material in the book well
____ (b) progress from basic to advanced concepts
____ (c) are helpful
____ (d) are distracting
____ (e) are too repetitive

5. Drills
____ (a) need illustrations
____ (b) are helpful
____ (c) are confusing
____ (d) are too advanced for beginning players
____ (e) are too simple for beginning players
____ (f) are easy to use
____ (g) are difficult to use

6. Instructional schedules are
____ (a) helpful
____ (b) easy to understand
____ (c) difficult to understand

7. Practice plans are
____ (a) helpful
____ (b) confusing
____ (c) too basic
____ (d) too advanced
____ (e) easy to use
____ (f) difficult to use

8. Coaching aids are
____ (a) helpful
____ (b) not helpful
____ (c) easy to use
____ (d) difficult to use

Yes No

____ **9. I feel more knowledgeable about coaching softball to beginning athletes than I did before reading this book.**

____ **10. I would like to attend a workshop or clinic covering the material presented in this book.**

Glossary

Backing up—Moving behind a base or player to field balls which get by the player.

Barrel—The fat section of the bat used to hit a pitched ball.

Basket catch—Catching with the glove pocket facing upward, held at or below the waist.

Battery—The duo comprised of the pitcher and catcher.

Blocking position—The ground ball fielding position of an outfielder; where the player kneels on the glove-side knee and places the mitt between the legs.

Breaking in—Conditioning a new glove by forming its shape and softening the leather.

Bunt—A method of hitting the ball by squaring with the pitcher and holding the bat so the ball is hit softly.

Checkpoint—A position used to evaluate a component or phase of a skill. A *checkpoint* of the pitching motion is the point of release.

Closed stance—The batting position in which the front foot is close to the inside of the batter's box, and the back foot is toward the outside of the batter's box.

Cut off—To catch a ball before it reaches a particular base. The shortstop may *cut off* a throw to third base.

Deep—To play the back part of the infield (for infielders), or the back part of the outfield (for outfielders).

Follow-through—The movement of the body resulting from a well-performed skill such as throwing, swinging, and batting.

Force-out—An out which occurs when a ball reaches a base before the runner does; in effect when a runner *must* advance to a base.

Grip—The way a ball, bat, or other implement is held.

Guard the line—Playing close to the first or third baseline to prevent a ball from being hit directly down the line.

Handle—The part of the bat the batter grips.

Holding on—Keeping a runner on or close to a base; preventing a runner from leading off or advancing to another base.

Hop-step—Throwing the ball by taking a short skip on the back foot; also called the skip and throw.

Infield fly rule—In effect when runners are on first and second or the bases are loaded, with less than 2 outs. Under these conditions, if a a pop-up is hit to the infield or shallow outfield, the batter is automatically out and the runners are not forced to advance.

Knob—The rounded part of the bat at the end of the handle which prevents the hand from slipping off.

Leading off—When a batter leaves a base in anticipation of running to the next base.

Open stance—The batting position in which the front foot is positioned toward the outside of the batters's box, and the back foot is positioned toward the inside of the batter's box.

Overhand throw—Throwing the ball with the arm swinging over the top of the body, as opposed to the sidearm throw; more accurate than the sidearm throw.

Pull—Hitting to the opposite part of the field. A right-handed batter *pulls* a ball to right field; a left-handed batter *pulls* a ball to left field.

Ready position—The position of a player preparing to play a ball.

Relay—Using several players to throw the ball over a long distance.

Rounding—Running around a base rather than stopping at a base.

Sidearm throw—Throwing the ball with the arm swinging around the side of the body, as opposed to the overhand throw; less accurate than the overhand throw and should be taught only after players can throw overhand well.

Shallow—Playing the front part of the infield (for infielders), or the front part of the outfield (for outfielders).

Shift—Moving the body weight when throwing, catching, and batting. Catchers *shift* to block wild throws.

Short hop—A thrown or hit ball which lands close to a fielder and hops or bounces up quickly.

Short fielder—The fourth outfielder on a slow-pitch softball team; also called a rover.

Slide—A controlled fall enabling runners to move into a base without standing up. *Sliding* is a good way to reach a base while avoiding a tag.

Slingshot—A windup in fast-pitch softball in which the arm swings backward and then forward, but does not revolve completely around the shoulder.

Square—To be in line and evenly facing a position, object, or person. To perform a bunt the batter turns *square* to the pitcher.

Stance—The upright, standing position of a fielder or batter; providing a solid base of support.

Steal—Advancing to another base without the ball being hit or a batter being walked. A runner *steals* second base.

Strategy—Plans and reasons for making plays. The defense uses certain playing *strategies* to control the offense.

Stride—Stepping into a throw or swing. The *stride* should be short and controlled.

Swing—Moving the arms around the body to throw a ball or swing a bat. The batting *swing* moves the bat around the body.

Tag up—Touching a base after a fly ball has been caught. Base runners must *tag up* on caught fly balls before running to the next base.

Take in—Catching a ball while fielding ground balls or fly balls; differs from a regular catch in that a *take-in* is specifically for catching a hit or rolling ball, not a thrown ball. The third baseman *takes in* a short-hop.

Time-out—Stopping the play of a game. Players and coaches can request a *time-out* by the umpire. If the umpire grants a *time-out*, play is suspended until the umpire calls, "Play ball!"

Track start—The recommended starting position for running from a base; one foot is placed against the base and the other foot is positioned comfortably in front of the base.

Windmill—A pitching windup in fast-pitch softball in which the arm swings up and around the body, completing one full revolution around the shoulder.

Notes

Notes

Notes

Notes